EDUCATION IN ANCIENT INDIA

Sri Garib Dass Oriental Series - No. 135

EDUCATION IN ANCIENT INDIA

S. M. RAKHE

SRI SATGURU PUBLICATIONS
A Division of
INDIAN BOOKS CENTRE
DELHI-INDIA

Published by :

Sri Satguru Publications
Indological and Oriental Publishers
A Division of
Indian Books Centre
40/5, Shakti Nagar,
Delhi-110007
(INDIA)

First Edition : Delhi 1992

ISBN - 81-7030-312-5

PRINTED IN INDIA

Dedicated to the Sacred feet of Shri Rama Krishna Paramahansa

CONTENTS

FOREWORD

Dr. Rakhe deserves congratulations in digging up the cultural ethos of the past, extending from the ages of Vedas to Puranas, in his monographs - Education in the Atharva- Veda, and, Education in the Vishnu-Purana. Taking support from scholars like S.C. Sarkar, Dr. Rakhe justifies the selection of Atharva Veda as his special study. Atharva Veda offers the most important source for the quest of educational research.

Dr. Rakhe has adopted a scientific technique in the selection and analysis of hymns.

The analysis focuses the relationship between the teacher and the pupil. The teaching learning continuum has a special meaning. The teacher in the past was more concerned about the well-being and prosperity of his pupil. The Vedic interpretation shows clearly that both the teacher and the pupil, according to Vedic dictates, are the vital components of educational process.

The formal and informal aspect of Vedic education are more important. That the child had to leave his parent's roof and take shelter in his Guru's house is an indication of a formal system. But the pupil's stay at his Guru's residence for the entire period of education includes all types of activities. It was living in a different family. This was an informal mode of teaching. Dr. Rakhe highlights the unique feature of the system. Dr Rakhe has hymn wise shown the functioning of the system.

The Central theme of study in Vishnu Purana is educational practice based on the particular educational philosophy. The bases according to Dr. Rakhe are not religious but moral. The moral norms as accepted by the then society determined the course of educating children and the youth of the times.

Dr. Rakhe has selected two episodes, viz., the Prahlad Episode and the episode of Ribhu and Nidagha to focus the teacher-pupil relationship. What is more important in the relationship is the authority of knowledge instead of the mere status-authority. The system as revealed here was rigorous. Education in those days was not a bed of roses. It was full of hard work and rigour. At the same time it was not Spartan in its function.

Dr. Rakhe has only brought the true spirit of ancient Indian educational system to light. The aim of education in those days was self-realization. In the process of self- realization the teacher-*Guru,* was a mere guide. Ribhu's illustration is an example of such a guide.

Dr. Rakhe's study of the Vishnu Purana in regard to the then prevailing educational practices will be of an immense value to the present educational practitioners.

When the New Educational Policy is stressing value and cultural heritage, the present investigation would provide an interesting reading material in the areas focused in the New Educational Policy and its Action Plan.

R.S. Trivedi
Ex. Vice Chancellor,
Bhavnagar University,
AHMEDABAD.

AN APPRECIATION

Self-study or svadhyaya has its own importance in every philosophy of education. Modern educational psychology gives perennial signifiance to the process of self-learning. Dr. Rakhe deserves congratulations for tracing the roots of svadhyaya in the vedic and post-vedic literature. Dr. Rakhe's study is very methodical and he has adopted scientific techniques in the analysis of the data.

Dr. Rakhe dicussed in detail the following topics in this monograph :

(i) Importance of knowledge

(ii) Importance of svadhyaya

(iii) Four Veda-Vratas

(v) Method of teaching Vedas and

(vi) The concept of Upakarma and Utsarjana as well as of Anadhyaya giving references to the original sources.

For these, he has consulted Vedas, Brahmanas, Upanishadas Pratishakhyas as well as Dharma sutras and smritis. He has supported his studies with the weightly works like Vedic Index. History of Dharmashastras, etc.

Anybody who wants to study the educational systems in ancient India will find interesting material in this scholarly work.

K. S. Shastri
Ex-Vice-Chancellor
Gujarat University
Ahmedabad

PREFACE

The present work is a collection of three monographs viz. Education in the Atharva-Veda, Education in the Vishnu-Purana and Svadhyaya in the Vedic and Post-Vedic Literature. The educational system of our land is first adumbrated in the Atharva-Veda. Of all the Vedas, the complex Atharva-Veda appears to be the most important source for the quest of educational information about very early ages. The Puranas are full of episodes having educational implications enlightening us on such vital points of education as teacher-student relationship, the true spirit of education etc. Svadhyaya has received perennial importance since the inception of educational system anywhere in the world. Svadhyaya has a very deep root in our ancient culture going back to the Rigveda. Our system considers studentship as a debt to Rishis or to culture and so the person who perpetually continues his Svadhyaya is designated as "Rishis : treasure warden." Mine is an humble attempt to explain and highlight these features of our ancient educational system.

It is a pleasant duty of the author to thank all those who have in any way assisted in the production of the present work. I am grateful to Dr. K. G. Desai, Ex. Director, University School of Psychology, Education and Philosophy, Gujarat University, for carefully going through the typescript and making a number of valuable suggestions. I am very much obliged to Prof. R.S. Trivedi, Ex. Vice Chancellor of Bhavnagar University for writing a Forword to this work. I am also indebted to Prof. K.S. Shastri, Ex. Vice Chancellor of Gujarat University for writing appreciation to the monograph - Svadhyaya in the Vedic and Post-Vedic Literature. I am also thankful to the librarians of Gujarat University, Ahmedabad and Government Sanskrit College Library, Indore (M.P.) for thier ready help during the period of my study. I am grateful to Mrs. Indira Chaudhari and Mr. K. K. Solanki for the proof-reading and also for preparing the Index. I am indebted to Indian Books Centre and owe my thanks for their interest in Indian Educational Thought and for consenting to publish the book.

S. M. Rakhe

Ahmedabad

THE BRAHMACHARIN AND HIS PRAYERS

Book XI/5/26

तानि कल्पद् ब्रह्मचारी सलिलस्य पृष्ठे तपोऽतिष्ठत् तप्यमानः समुद्रे।
स स्नातो बभ्रुः पिङ्गलः पृथिव्यां बहु रोचते।।

Book VII/61/1

यदग्ने तपसा तप उपतप्यामहे तपः।
प्रियाः श्रुतस्य भूयास्मायुष्मन्तः सुमेधसः।।

Book VI/133/4

श्रद्धाया दुहिता तपसोऽधि जाता स्वस ऋषिणां भूतकृतां बभूव।
सा नो मेखले मतिमा धेहि मेधामथो नो धेहि तप इन्द्रियं च।।

Book VI/108/3

यां मेधामृभवो विदुर्यां मेधामसुरा विदुः।
ऋषयो भद्रां मेधां यां विदुस्तां मय्या वेशयामसि।।

EDUCATION IN THE ATHARVA-VEDA

INTRODUCTION

The Atharva-veda is a comparatively late addition to three ancient Vedas which formed the foundation of the early culture of the Indian people. Sayana in his commentary on the Atharva-veda has very strongly advocated the importance of the Atharva in ritual performances (1/I/:4-6). Atharva-veda derives its name from a Rishi of indefinitely remote antiquity named Atharvan, who is referred to in the Rigveda as the first priest who produced fire by attrition, established communication between men and Gods (by sacrifice) and overcame hostile demons by means of miraculous powers *(6/I/iii)*. To the decendants of the Atharvan, associated with the members of two other ancient priestly families Angirases and the Bhrigus, the collected hymns - called also the Athavangirasas and the Bhrigvangirases were, it is said, originally revealed. According to Bloomfield Atharva-veda consists of atharvan and angiras matter and the term atharvan refers to the auspicious practices of the Veda while the term angiras refers to hostile sorcery practices of the Veda (3:xviii).

The Mantras of the Atharva-veda were generally meant for application at humbler Grihya sacrifices of common people evolved round the plain and simple primitive fire cult. It reveals the religion practised by the common people - the average middle-class agriculturist. A devout believer in the Gods, he spent his substance on simple ceremonies and performed sacrifices with humble offerings which he could well afford. His principal concern was the well-being of his family and friends. He prayed for plentiful harvest and for thriving and multiplying cattle.

Brahma-veda is another term used for the Veda on the ground that (1) it is the Veda of the Brahman or chief sacrificial priest whose duty was to supervise and direct the whole sacrifice, (2) it deals with the knowledge of Prayers (Brahmani). and (3) it teaches the wisdom of Brahman which ultimately leads man to the final liberation. Because of these specific features the Veda has drawn keen attention of the scholars of indology.

In the view of Radha Kumud Mookerji the educational system is first adumbrated in the Atharva-veda and "First there is the ceremony of Upanayana by which the teacher, acharya, initiates the pupil, brahmachari, into a new life described as second birth, whence he becomes a dvija, twice born" *(9/I/:128)* S.C. Sarkar stated that of all the Vedas, the complex Atharva-veda appeared to be the most important source for the quest of educational information about very early ages (12:1).

The present study of the Atharvavedic hymns having educational indications was undertaken with a view to analysing them and to highlighting their educational significance.

METHOD

The main source of the data was the Original Sanskrit Text of the Atharva-veda with Sayana's Commentary published by Vishveshvarananda Vedic Research Institute, Hoshiyarpur. The commentaries and translations of the Atharva-veda by Whitney, Griffith and Bloomfield were of immense help to the author for the English rendering of the hymns and also in their analysis.

The hymns were selected on the basis of their employment in the investiture of initiation and that of in the end of student life ceremony by the Kaushika-Sutra or their application in the rites as interpreted by Sayana and also on the basis of their contents. In all forty-seven hymns from different books of the Atharva-veda were selected for the study, and the details regarding their application under different heads and their occurrence in the books of Atharva-veda are given in the following table:

Table of The Hymns

No.	Heads	Book No.									Total Hymns
		I	II	III	IV	VI	VII	VIII	XI	XIX	
I	Initiation	1,9		8	1, 9, 10, 13	38, 40, 48, 53 56, 58, 68, 69, 71, 108, 133	32, 33, 53 54, 56, 57(i), 61, 66(68) 67(69), 82	1,2 43,	5 64,	4, 40, 68	34
II	Student Life	33, 34		30		1, 64, 94	12, 16, 105			71	10
III	End of Student Life	30	29							72	3
	Total										47

ANALYSIS

I. HYMNS REFERRING TO THE UPANAYANA CEREMONY

Book I, Hymn 1:

The hymn is a prayer addressed to Vachaspati for divine help, favour and illumination *6/I/1)*.

Sayana in his commentary on the Sukta states that on the auspicious day of Upanayana, the Brahmacharin, desirous of wisdom (intellect) should perform oblation of ghee[1] by employing the Mantras of the Sukta *(1/I/30)*. According to the Kaushika-

1. Keshava explains in his Paddhati,

'अथ ब्रह्मचार्युपनयनानन्तरं मेधाजननमन्त्रैरायुष्यमन्त्रैश्चाज्यं जहुयात्'

(4:359-31)

Sutra this hymn is to be employed for the production of wisdom (Madhajanana) ceremony *(4 (57-31):160)* The same Sukta is employed in the ceremony for the welfare of the Vedic student. It is used further, with various other passages, in that of entrance upon Vedic study *(13/I/1).*

In the first verse, Vachaspati is prayed to assign the strength and power of those Gods (twenty-one in number) who go about, bearing all forms. In the second Vachaspati is invited again with divine mind to repose with the devotee and to bestow on him the sacred knowledge of the Vedas.

Sayana states that as the first verse is to be employed for the ceremony for the production of wisdom, and as only the Lord of speech (that is the Vedas) could confer such ability, the prayer is addressed to Brahma *(1/I/:36).* Whitney *(13/I/:1)* and Griffith *(6/I/1),* render the word Vachaspati as Lord of speech.

In the second verse the Lord of speech is also addressed as Vasoshpati. Sayana takes it as (i) Vasupati that is Lord of wealth, and also as (ii) Prajapati (Vasaka-Prana) *(1/I/:38).* Griffith renders it as Lord of Treasure *(6/I/:2),* and Whitney as Lord of good *(13/I/:2).* According to Sayana as the verse is employed in the production of wisdom ceremony, Shrutam means Vedas learnt from the teacher and the prayer is for the retention of that knowledge of the Vedas *1/I/:38).* Griffith renders it as knowledge, that which is heard (from the beginning) -Veda *(6/I/:2).* Whitney takes it as what is heard (sacred learning) *(13/I/:2).*

In the third and fourth verse the Lord of speech is invoked to confirm the knowledge in the prayerful.

According to Sarkar the hymn gives some of the formulae which were used on a student's entrance upon the Vedic study with special objects of ensuring his retention of sacred learning *(12:2-3).*

On the basis of its contents and its employment in the ceremonies like initiation, production of wisdom, and welfare of the Vedic student, the hymn has become a significant source of educational information of the time. In the age of later Samhitas the whole of the Vedic literature was looked upon as 'Shruti' or revealed literature. The Vedic literature must therefore have formed the main body of study and the vital part of education. So the process of imparting the knowledge of the sacred hymnology and sacrificial ritual must have become more and more systematized during this age *(7:454)*. The prayers in the Atharva-veda for liturgical employment at the ceremony of initiation can stand as a testimony to this contention.

Book I, Hymn 9:

The hymn has also been employed for the ceremony of initiation *(1/I/:74-75)*. The hymn with seven others is employed by a teacher[1] at the reception of a Vedic student.

The hymn is a prayer for earthly and heavenly success. The first two are addressed to Gods - Vasus, Indra, Pushan, Varuna, Mitra and Agni etc. The last two are addressed to Agni.

In the first hemistich of the first verse the gods are invoked to maintain the prayerful in riches and in the second Adityas and Vishvedevas are prayed to maintain him in superior lustre.

In the first hemistich of the second verse the gods are invoked so that the light (heavenly as well as earthly) be at his command. In the second they are invoked to exalt the devotee to highest firmament and for his supermacy over his rivals.

The third and fourth verse are the prayers to Agni in which Agni is invoked to exalt the prayerful to the highest heaven and for his supremacy over his kinsmen and rivals.

In Bloomfield's view the Kaushika-Sutra employs the hymn in practices designed to confer glory, lusture upon any one at all. The hymn is recited along with a list of others "at the investiture of the young twice born.*(3:239-40)*. Sarkar treats the hymn as one of many passages illustrating the sort of professional utterances at the reception of Vedic student *(12:7)*. The hymn is uttered by the teacher at the initiation ceremony for the formal acceptance of the pupil. Here the teacher entrusts the earthly as well as the heavenly success of the pupil to the care of the dieties like Agni, Varuna, Indra, Pushan, Adityas etc.

---

1. Kaushika states : एनं प्राञ्चमवस्थाप्य दक्षिणेन पाणिना नाभिदेशेऽभिसंस्तभ्य जपति - 'अस्मिन् वसु वसवो धारयन्तु'।

(4(55, 16, i) 154 - 55)

Scholiast: पूर्वाभिमुखं ब्रह्मचारिणमुपवेश्य, नाभिदेशं संस्पृश्य संस्तभ्य - (आयुष्यगण) जपति आचार्यः।

(4 : 359)

Book III, Hymn 8:

The hymn is a prayer for authority. Sayana states that the Sukta is employed in the ceremony for the reception of a Vedic student and for the generation of wisdom[1] *(1/I/:302)*. Griffith takes it as a charm to secure the submission, love, and fidelity of kinsmen *(6/I/:90)*.

The first verse is addressed to Mitra, Varuna, Vayu and Agni to make the realm tranquil and exalted.

In the first hemistich of the second verse the deities are invoked to hear the words of the prayerful and accept them. In the second hemistich Aditi is prayed for getting the centre position among the kinsmen.

The third is a prayer addressed to Soma and Adityas to get prominence in the contest and to get love of the kinsmen.

The first hemistich of the fourth verse is addressed to the kinsmen requesting them to stay together and the rest to the Vishvedevas to grant the prayerful his desires.

The fifth and sixth are addressed to the kinsmen to receive their fidelity.

The employment of the hymn in the educational context suggests that with this prayer the pupil wishes to secure harmony and friendship with the fellow students. He also wishes to be in the centre position in his group and also desires to win the contest but he wants to achieve all these with divine grace hence he needs qualities, blessed with which he may get pre-eminence but at the same time he wants the sacrificial fire lighted by his fellowmen to send forth its splendour for very long and that too with their consentient. So it is a prayer for the decent corporate life in which healthy competition has its proportionate value.

Book IV Hymn 1:

Sayana states that the Sukta is employed in the beginning of the study of the Vedas to avoid obstructions and to get pre-

1. Kaushika-Sutra (55.17-18 and also 55.1 note), Scholiast (4 : 313 10.19 note)

eminence in the scholastic debates *(1/I/:401). According to Whitney Sayana enjoins only the use of the first verse of the hymn for recitation on the occasions (13/I/:142, also 4 (139.10):927).* Here only the first verse of the hymn is discussed. The hymn is a brahmodyam or enunciation in designedly enigmatical language of cosmogonical and mystico-theological doctrine *(6/I/129f).* The first verse runs as:

(1) The Brahman that was first generated in the east, Vena disclosed bright flashes from the summit, he disclosed his deepest, nearest revelations, womb of the non-existent and existent.

Sayana renders Brahman as Surya : Vena as luminous deity *(1/I/402-03).* Griffith takes Brahman as prayer and Vena as the early sun *(6/I/:129).*

Vena is referred to in the first hemistich of the first verse of the Book II as - Vena beholds that highest which lies hidden wherein this all resumes one form and fashion'. Griffith states that Vena 'the loving sun' of Rigveda I, 83, 5, Kantah or the 'the beloved' is said by the scholiast to be madhyasthano devah-a God of the middle region of the air. He is apparently, the Sun as he rises in the mists of the morning *(6/I/:41). Griffith further explains that the prayer (IV.I) originated in the eastern heaven, when the early Sun (Vena), first rose in his glory he poured forth the type of human prayer, his morning song of joy and praise (6/I/:129).* The sun is first born of heaven and earth, and his birth is the type of all subsequent generation.

The Sun and the Sun-born Goddess Savitri are worshipped to stimulate talent.

Book IV, Hymn 9:

The hymn is used *(4 (58.8):161) with the binding on of an ointment-amulet, in a ceremony for long life of the vedic pupil after his initiation (13/I/:158). While reciting the hymn, an amulet of salve is fastened upon the pupil.*

The hymn is addressed to a precious ointment, for protection from all sorts of evil and for the acquisition of wealth. The mountain Trikakud is the source from which the salve is derived. It is also said to be derived from Yamuna. The sixth and seventh verse run like this:

(6) From lying speech, from evil dream, evil deed, and also from foulness, from the evil eye of the enemy, from this protect us, O Salve.

(7) Knowing this, O Salve, I shall speak the truth, avoid falsehood. May I obtain horses and cattle and thy soul, O man.

The Salve is expected to protect the pupil from all sorts of evil but it becomes imperative for the child to be truthful so that he may pray for wealth.

Book IV, Hymn 10:

The hymn is employed in connection with a practice for bestowing long life and prosperity upon the young disciple after the investiture *(3:383)*. While reciting IV, 10 an amulet of pearl is fastened upon the youth *(4 (58.9) :161- 62)*..

The hymn is addressed to the pearl and its shell as an amulet-Shanka-mani according to Sayana *(1/I/:437)* bestowing long life and prosperity. In addresses to amulets, the origin of the shell is glorified. It was produced from the rain that fell into the sea from the windy sky, and the iridescent hues of its lining came from the bright flashes of the lightning *(6/I/:142-43)*. The seventh verse runs as:

(7) The bone of the gods turned into pearl, that endowed with soul moveth in the waters. That do I fasten upon thee unto life, strength, longevity, unto a life lasting a hundred autumns, May the (amulet) of pearl protect thee.

The vedic teacher seems to be very much concerned about the well-being and prosperity of his pupil but he is also very much anxious to see that his pupil imbibes qualities like truthfulness etc. as virtues are basic to all prosperity.

Book IV, Hymn 13:

The hymn is employed in the ceremonies for long life that follow the initiation *(4(58:3,4,11) 161-62). Sayana commenting on the first verse of the hymn states that " O Gods, make this initiated pupil aware of his holy-duties so that he may not deflect from them. Let the pupil receive the excellent fruit of learning (1/I/:451).* While reciting specifically the sixth and seventh verse the seer touches the pupil for his good health and well- being. The two verses run as:

(6) This is my felicitous hand, this my more felicitous one, this my all-healing one, and this makes whole with gentle touch.

(7) The tongue that leads the voice precedes. Then without ten-fold-branching hands-with these two healers of disease, we stroke thee with a soft caress.

Book VI, Hymn 38:

The hymn belongs to Varchasya Ganas. Varchas – Sayana takes it as Tejas *(1/II/:695)*, Griffith as energy *(6/I/:265)*, Whitney as brilliancy *(13/I/:309)* and Bloomfield as lustre *(3:116)*.. The object of the hymn (along with 39) and the practices connected with it is to endow a king or a pupil etc. with Varchas and more particularly to transfer to him the Varchas inherent in men, animals and brilliant substances. Both the hymns are rubricated in the course of practices at the initiation of pupils to the study of the Vedas *(4(139.5):296)*. The rite is termed as Utsarjana that is rite of dedication performed on entering upon Vedic study.

The Hymn is a prayer for lustre and power. Here the pupil prays to the blest Goddess-Aditi to approach him in union with the lustre and power of the fierce, virile and noble animals (the lion, the tiger, the serpent etc.) and that of the warrior and the Brahmana along with the lustre and power of deities like Agni, Varuna, Surya etc.

The Vedic educator wants to bless his pupil not only with the noble qualities but also with physical and material excellences. Strength and prosperity go together. Without strength, where is excellence?. Without excellence, there can be no vigour nor heroism.

Book VI, Hymn 40:

Sayana notes its application according to the Kaushika-Sutra

(4(139.7):296-97) in the rite for beginning Vedic study. He enjoins to offer ghee while reciting the hymn in the act of Upanayana *(1/II/:698).*

The hymn is a prayer for freedom from fear that is for peace and security. It prays for the safety and peace of the land, invokes deities to bestow fearlesness on the prayerful and also for the safety from the wrath of kings.

Book VI, Hymn 48:

The hymn is employed in the initiation for delivering a staff to one consecrated or to a Vedic student. The teacher gives the (staff to the pupil and he accepts it *(13/I/:316).* A staff was given by the Acharya to the pupil who accepted it for the sake of long life, of holy lustre and holiness *(11:134).*

The first verse of the hymn is adressed to Agni who from his rapid motion in his form of lightning is called the hawk *(6/I/:271), who is prayed for the welfare of Yanja.*

The second is addressed to Ribhu - the representative of the three Ribhus, the sages who through their assiduous performance of good works obtained divinity and the third is addressed to Indra for the welfare of Yajna.

Book VI, Hymn 53:

The Hymn is applied in the Upanayana, while reciting VI, 53, 3 along with others the water bowl is consecrated in which the pupil sees his face *(1/II/:719).*

The hymn is for protection and is addressed to various Gods. It is a prayer for recovery and preservation of health and security.

Sayana enjoins that it is used in the production of wisdom ceremony with VI.108 to accompany the partaking of some dish (milk-rice) and waiting upon the Sun *(1/II/:718-19).*

Book VI, Hymn 56:

This is used in a rite for welfare *(4(50-17):146). It is also used along with various others in the ceremony for commencing Vedic study (4(139.8):297).*

The hymn is a charm against snakes, but the Kaushika-Sutra gives it a pragmatic turn: the practice is designed to keep serpents away from the premises *(3:487)*

Book VI, Hymn 58:

It is used in the introduction of Vedic study *(4(139.15):297). It appears with various others, with an oblation to Agni 1/I/:729).* It is a prayer for power and glory. It has three verses. The third runs as:

(3) Indra and Agni were renowned, famous was Soma at his birth:

So too am I illustrious, most glorious of all that is.

Book VI Hymn 68:

The Hymn is employed in the Upanayana at the beginning of the whole ceremony with the direction "do as directed in the text" *(13/I/332).*

It is a charm to accompany the act of shaving. It might be connected with the diksha, the religious ceremony of initiation. It has three verses. the third runs as:

(3) With what razor the knowing Savitar shaved (the head) of King Soma, of Varuna, therewith, O Brahman, shave ye this man, be he rich, in horses, kine and children.

This was a samskara which consecrated the first shaving of the student's beard.

Book VI, Hymn 69:

This hymn is employed by the Kaushika-Sutra *(4(10,24)32)* at the end of the madhajanana ceremony with other mantras on rising and wiping the face; further, in ceremony on beginning Vedic study with others.

The hymn is a prayer for power and glory. It has three verses, the third runs as:

(3) In me be strength, in me be fame, in me the power of sacrifice; Prajapati establish that in me as firm as light in heaven.

Book VI, Hymn 71:

The hymn is employed by the Kaushika-sutra *(4(45,17)125-26) with others in a rite for obviating ill effects from acceptance of gifts and the like, also in the (4(57.29-30):160)* Upanayana, accompanying an offering by the pupil from the food obtained by begging.

The hymn is an expiatory prayer to obviate any impropriety, such as greed and worldliness, on the part of the Brahmana or teacher who receives gift or absence of sacredness in the gift itself. It is recited along with others upon the receipt of the dakshina: the begging Brahmachari offers, while reciting the hymn, the fruits of his mendicancy: the firewood, which he has begged is put on the fire in the evening and in the morning, while reciting this hymn *(3:494)*.

It is a Brahmanical prayer at the receipt of gifts, It has three verses. the second and third run as:

(2) The gift that has come to me by sacrifice, or without sacrifice, bestowed by the Fathers, granted by men, through which my heart, as it were, lights up with joy-may Agni the priest, render that an auspicious offering.

(3) The food that I, O Gods, improperly consume, (the food) I promise, intending to give of it, or not to give of it, by the might of mighty Vaishvanara (Agni) may (that) food be for me auspicious and full of honey *(3:196-97)*.

The teacher may accept wealth but it should be in accordance with social justice and morality. He must be free from avarice and worldly desires.

Book VI, Hymn 108:

The Hymn is employed in the medhajanana ceremony

4(10:20-21):32) and also *(4(57:28):160) in the Upanayana with worship of Agni.*

This specifically is a prayer for wisdom (true in its contents). It has five verses; they run as:

(1) Intelligence, come first to us with kine, with horses; thou with rays of the sun, art our worshipful and holy one.

(2) The first, devout Intelligence, lauded by sages, sped by prayer; trusted by Brahmachari, for the favour of the gods I call.

(3) That excellent Intelligence which Ribhus know and Asuras; Intelligence which sages know, we cause to enter into me.

(4) The intelligence which the creative Rishis, which the men endowed with wisdom know, with that intelligence, do thou, O Agni, make me wise this day.

(5) Intelligence at eve, at morn, Intelligence at noon of day, with the sun's rays, by the speech we plant in us intelligence.

The medhajanana ceremony speaks of the high concern of the Vedic educators about the intellectual well-being of the pupil. The hymn is symbolical of intelligence-a prayer to stimulate talent.

Book VI, Hymn 133:

The hymn is employed in the Upanayana. The verses four and five of the hymn are used in the ceremony *(4(57.1):158) with tying on the sacred girdle. The hymn has five verses. The fourth and fifth run as.*

(4) She hath become, Faith's daughter, sprung from tapas, the sister of the world-creating Rishis, as such, O Girdle, give us thought and wisdom, give us religious zeal and mental vigour.

(5) Thou whom primeval Rishis girt about them, they who made the world, as such do thou encircle me, O Girdle, for long days of life.

(4) Sayana takes Bhutakritam Rishinam as world– creating Rishis beginning with Marichi, Atri, Matim as intellect having control over future, Medham as an intellect able to conserve the wisdom of Vedas *(1/II/856)*. Griffith takes Bhutakritam as world creating, tapas as religious zeal, and Indriyam as mental vigour *(6/I/320)*. Withney takes Bhutakritam as being-making and Indriyam as Indra's power *(13/I/:381)*.

In his prayer the pupil prays for intellect, knowledge, tapas, mental vigour along with Rishihood.

Book VII Hymns 32, 33, 53:

The three hymns are employed in the ceremony of initiation *(4(58.3.11.; 57.22.25; 55.17) 160-62,153)*. The thirty two is a prayer for long life, addressed to Agni and the thirty three for long life, children and riches addressed to various gods. The fifty three with others is addressed by the teacher to the pupil in the ceremony of initiation. It is also a prayer for long-life.

The Ayushya hymns-hymns belonging to Ayushya-Gana are very uniform in character. They are generally employed at the ceremony of Upanayana.

Book VII Hymn 54 [56, 57 (i)]:

The Kaushika Sutra employs this in a rite for the gaining of wealth by teachers *(4(42:9.10) 115-16)*. Sayana states that the verse 54, I, is used for avoidance of obstructions in gaining of wealth by teachers (1/II/:947). According to scholiast (note to 55.15 4:359) it is used in the initiation as one looks at the Sun and asks his protection for the boy. In Griffith's view this hymn is a charm to obtain knowledge of the Veda. The two verses of the hymn run as:

(1) We worship holy Verse and Song, by which they carry out their acts; shining in order's seat these twain present the sacrifice to Gods.

(2) As I have asked about Verse, Song, Sacrifice, strength, force, Yajus-text

So never let this lore that I have sought forsake me, Lord of Might *(6/I/:352-53)*.

Griffith renders Richam as Rigvedic hymn, Saman as of the Sama- veda, Karmani Kurvate as men perform the rite of divine worship, sadasi-a certain shed erected in the sacrificial enclosure *(6/I/352f).*

(2) Apraksham — asked my teacher, Yajus — Yajus-text (sacrificial formula in that Veda), Shachipati — Lord of power, Shachi — originally power of Indra, Veda — Sacred lore (6/I/353f).)

Book VII, Hymn 61:

The hymn is employed inthe medhajanana (4 (10.22) : 32) and in the ceremony of reception of a Vedic student *(4(57:23) 159-60).*

The hymn is a prayer for success in penance and for the acquisition of sacred knowledge and its fruits. It has two verses:

(1) Since Agni, with our fervent zeal we undergo penance, may we be dear to Sacred Lore, may we be wise and live long lives.

(2) O Agni, we perform penance, we undergo austerity; so listening to Holy Lore may we grow wise and full of days.

It is through 'tapas' that the Vedic student wants to achieve knowledge and propitiate his teacher. It is with discipline and fervour that the student becomes darling of Mother Shruti-the Sacred Lore.

Book VII, Hymn 66 (68):

Sayana connects the hymn with the prescriptions as to the time of study or refraining from study of the sacred texts referring to the Apastamba Sutra in the Svadhyaya chapter (XV.21.8), and regards it as a charm for recovering what has been lost by being learned under wrong circumstances-in cloudy weather, in sight of green barley, within hearing of cattle etc. *(1/II/:972). The hymn has only one verse:*

(1) If it was in the wind or air's mid region, if it was in the trees or in the bushes, what the cattle heard uttered- Let that Brahmana (Vedas) come again to us.

Thus the hymn is a prayer for recovery of sacred knowledge.

Book VII, Hymn 67 (69):

The hymn is employed in the Vedic student ceremonies *(4:159 (57:8)*, when supplying the place of a staff lost or destroyed *(1/II/:969)*, further in the Upanayana, in the reception of girdle and staff (4(56:1-2notes):155). It has one verse:

(1) May sense return to me again, my spirit, return my property and knowledge; let the fires of the sacred hearth again officiate just here in their respective stations.

The Hymn is a prayer for recovery of sense etc.

Book VII, Hymn 82:

The verses 2-6 of the hymn are emloyed in the Upanayana ceremony, accompany the laying of five pieces of fuel in renewing a lost fire *(13/I/:448: 1/I/1009)*. The hymn is a praise and prayer to Agni. The second verse runs as:

(2) I seize in me Agni at first with splendour and with might, in me I put progeny, in me life-time-hail in me Agni.

Book VIII, Hymns 1, 2:

Both the hymns are employed in the Upanayana, According to Sayana the first two Suktas are called Artha Suktas which are recited in the initiation by the teacher by touching the student's navel and with others for long life *(1/II/1060: 13/II/472)*.

This is an almost impassioned prayer for long life. It is employed in the course of investiture of initiation in certain special ceremonies (Brahmanoktam, and Rishihastaka) calculated to ensure longevity *(3:569-70)*.

Book XI Hymn 5:

The hymn is a glorification of the Brahmacharin-Vedic – student. It is cited also at the beginning of Gopatha Brahmana – the chapter on Brahmacharya (8:23). It is not quoted in the Kaushika or the Vaitana Sutra but the scholiast to Kaushika-Sutra 55.18 prescribes verse 3 in the Upanayana *(4 (55.18) 6f:155)*. Whitney states that Deussen entitles the hymn "The Brahman-pupil as incarnation of Brahm" *(13/II/636)*. In Bloomfield's view the Rigvedic hymn X, 136 contains the glorification of the Sun as a muni, a solitary ascetic: the present hymn may be understood best from a similar starting point. The sun is here for the nonce imagined as a Bramacharin, engaged in the practice of his holy vows, next, by an easy transition, all the functions and powers of the Brahmacharin are made the basis of a momentary cosmogonic and philosophical account of the origin and existence of the universe *(3:626)*. The hymn contains twenty six verses:

(1) The Brahmacharin moves stirring both hemispheres of the world, in him the Gods are harmonized. He holds firmly the heavens and the earth, *he fills the teacher with fervour (Tapas).*

(2) The fathers, the divine folk and all the Gods individually follow the Brahmacharin. The Gandharvas went after him, six thousand three hundred and thirty three. *He fills all the gods with fervour.*

(3) *When the Master receives the Brahmacharin as a disciple (taking him in charge), he places him as an embryo within. He bears him in his belly for three nights; when he is born the Gods convene to see him.*

(4) This earth is (his first) piece of firewood, the second is the heaven, and the atmosphere also he fills with (the third) piece of firewood. The Brahmacharin fills the worlds *with his firewood, his girdle, his asceticism,* and *his tapas* (fervour).

(5) The Brahmacharin prior to Brahma was born: *robed in heat, by tapas he arose.* From him sprung Brahmanam and the highest Brahma, all the Gods together with immortality.

(6) The Brahmacharin advances, *kindled by the firewood, clad in black-antelope skin, consecrate, long-bearded. Swiftly he passes from eastern to northern sea: grasping the worlds he repeatedly brings them anear him.*

(7) The Brahmacharin begetting the Brahman (Prayer), the waters, the world, Prajapati, Parameshthin and Viraj, and having become an embryo in the womb of immoratality, having forsooth, become Indra, pierced the Asuras.

(8) *The Master fashioned* these two hemispheres of the world, the broad and deep, earth and heaven. *These the Brahmacharin guards with his tapas;* in him the Gods are harmonized.

(9) This broad earth and the heaven the Brahmacharin first brought hither *as alms.* Having made them(both) into two sticks of firewood he reveres them; upon them all beings have been founded.

10) *Both treasures of Brahman (Sacred Lore) lie hidden, one is on the hither side, the other on the farther side of the back of the heavens; these the Brahmacharin protects by his tapas; he makes this solely his own as knowing Brahma.*

(11) Hitherward one, hence from the earth the other, do the two Agnis come together between these two hemispheres (of the world). To them adhere the rays firmly; the Brahmacharin by his tapas enters into the (rays).

(12) Thundering, shouting, ruddy-hued, and pallid, he bears along the earth great manly vigour. The Brahmacharin sprinkles seed upon the back of the earth; by that live the four directions.

(13) Into fire, the Sun, the Moon Matarishvan and the waters, the Brahmacharin places the firewood; their gleams separately go into the clouds, from them come sacrificial butter, the Purusha, rain and water.

(14) *The Master is death, Varuna, Soma, the plants and milk, the clouds were the warriors: by these this light has been brought hither.*

(15) *Varuna having become Master, makes his own the entire ghee. Whatever he desired from Prajapati, that the Brahmacharin furnished as a friend (Mitra) from his own atman.*

(16) The Brahmacharin is the Master. The Brahmacharin is Prajapati. Prajapati rules. Viraj became Indra, The ruler.

(17) Through Brahmacharyam, through tapas the king protects his kingdom. *The teacher by (his own) Brahmacharyam seeks (finds) the Brahmacharin.*

(18) *Through Brahmacharyam the maiden obtains a young husband,* through Brahmacharyam the steer, the horse seeks to obtain fodder.

(19) *Through Brahmacharyam, through tapas, the Gods drove away death.* Indra, forsooth, by his Brahmacharyam brought heaven ('s lustre) to the Gods.

(20) The plants, that which was and shall be, day and night, the forest tree, the year along with seasons have sprung from the Brahmacharin.

(21) The earthly and the heavenly animals, the wild and the domestic, the wingless and the winged (creatures) have sprung from the Brahmacharin.

(22) All the creatures of Prajapati distinctly carry breath in themselves. All these the Brahma that is stored within the Brahmacharin protects.

(23) Piled up on high, but never yet ascended, that power of deities moves brightly shining, from that has sprung the Brahmanam (Brahmanical life), the highest Brahma, and all the Gods, together with immortality.

(24-25) The Brahmacharin carries the radiant Brahman, wherein all Gods are woven. Generating in-breathing and out- breating as well as through-breathing; speech, mind, heart, Brahma, and intellect, do thou bestow on us the sight, hearing, glory, food, semen, blood and belly.

(26) Fashioning these things, *the Brahmacharin stood in the water kindled with tapas. He, when he has bathed in the ocean, shines exceedingly upon the earth, brown and ruddy.*

Commentary

(I) Sayana explains Brahmacharin as the one who is diligently devoted to the study of the Vedas, Ishnan as with his tapas, Charati as behaves according to his discipline, Piparti as protects — with his holy life the pupil protects his teacher *(1/III/:1365)*. Whitney and Bloomfield render piparti as fills *(13/II/636,4:214)*. Whitney and Griffith take tapas as fervour *(13/II/636,6/II/68)*) and Bloomfield takes it as creative fervour *(3:214)*.

(II) Sayana concludes his discussion of the verse thus: The Brahmacharin protects all the Gods with his holy discipline *(1/II/1365)*.

(III) Sayana takes the first hemistich as-the teacher receives the Brahmacharin as a disciple and places him as a foetus in his body of learning. He quotes the Apastamba Dharmasutra as—

स हि विद्यातस्तं जनयति । तच्छ्रेष्ठं जन्म । शरीरमेव मातापितरौ जनयतः ।

(1/I/:1366). "Acharya performs for the disciple the part of a spiritual second mother; and by the initiation ceremony the youth is regenerated or born anew" *(6/II/68f)*. Whitney maintains that Upa-ni was probably already a technical term (for receive as pupil, initiate) *(13/II/636)*.

(IV) Sayana explains the second hemistich as the Brahmacharin protects the worlds with his firewood, his girdle (Maunji of kush-grass), his asceticism and tapas: therefore placing firewood on the sacrificial fire etc, were essential imperatives for the Brahmacharin *(1/II/1366)*. "Samit-this log", explains Griffith, "Part of the ceremony consists in Brahmacharin's placing fuel on the sacrificial fire". He further renders Mekhala as zone and takes it either sacrificial cord or girdle-first assumed at initiation *(6/II/69f)*.

(VI) Sayana explains the first hemistich as the Brahmacharin kindled by placing the firewood on the sacrificial fire, clad in the black-antelope skin, consecrated by the holy discipline, with long beard that is well-established in the Brahmacharya-vow leads his way of life *(1/II/1367)*. According to Griffith the black-antelope skin is prescribed for religious student. This skin is one of the symbols of Brahmanical worship and civilization *(6/II/52f,69f)*. The term Ajina refers generally to the skin of a gazelle *[1/I/607(V,21,7)]*.

(IX) Griffith explains Bhiksham as with reference to the poverty of the Brahmachari who lives on the gifts of the pious *(6/II/69)*.

(X) Sayana explains the other Nidhi as the Vedas, Guha as Guhayam that is in the heart of the teacher: Vidvan as knower of the secret of the Vedas *(1/III/:1369)*. Griffith takes two Nidhis as both treasuries of sacred lore. He renders the second hemistich as he makes all his own as knowing Brahma and quotes Muir, "Wise, he appropriates that divine knowledge as his exclusive portion *(6/II/70f)*.

(XI) The two Agnis are explained by Sayana as the fire of the Sun and the terrestrial fire *(1/III/1369)*. Griffith explains them as lightning and terrestrial fire and adds "but the sense is not clear"*(6/II/70f)*.

(XIV) Sayana in order to put some sense into identification of the teacher with death and Varuna, regards it alluding to the instruction of Nachiketas by Death (Yama) and of Bhrigu by Varuna *(1/III/1371)*.

(XV) Sayana states at the end of his commentary on this verse that the Brahmacharin or disciple should satisfy his teacher by bringing him the desired gift, So he takes Varuna as the teacher and Mitra as his disciple)*(1/III/1371-72)*.

(XVII) Commenting on the second hemistich Sayana states that the teacher too seeks a disciple by the virtue of his holy life. Only to the teachers who are established in holy discipline the pupils approach *(1/III/1372)*. Griffith's note on the verse is very interesting. He renders Brahmacharya as self-restraint and explains that it means religious study in general, The self-restraint and purity are enjoined upon all religious students and are regarded as pre-eminent virtues. He also states a graphic story that illustrates the great virtue ascribed to Brahmacharya from the Taittiriya Brahmana *(iii,10,11,3)* : Bharadvaja practised Brahmacharya during three lives. Indra, approaching him when he was lying decayed and old, said; "Bharadvaja, if I give thee a fourth life, what wilt thou do with it?" He answered, "I will use it only to practise Brahmacharya". He further quotes Alfred Hillebrandt, "Vedic poet's fancy has represented the mutual relations of the Sun and the Moon in those of the Acharya and the Brahmacharin. Especially in stanza three, the Acharya is the Sun who devours the dying Moon and Keeps him within him during three nights *(6/II/:70-71f)*.

(XXII) Commenting on the second hemistich sayana states that the study of the Vedas through Brahmacharya guards all the creatures *(1/II/1374)*.

(XXIV) Sayana explains the first hemistich as the Brahmacharin bears the shining wisdom of the Vedas, so all the Gods dwell in him. He quotes the Taittiriya Aranyaka —

यावतीर्वै देवतास्ता सर्वा वेदविदि ब्राह्मणे वसन्ति । (2, 15, 1)

(1/II/1375).

Book XIX Hymn 4:

The hymn is employed in the Medhajanana ceremony *(1/IV/1795)*. It is addressed to various divinities. It is a prayer, accompanying sacrifice, for the attainment of a wish. The hymn has four verses. The second and fourth run as:

(2) Heavenly fortunate design, do I put forward; let the mother of thought be easy of invocation for us; to what expectation I go, be it entirely mine; may I find it entered into (my) mind.

(4) Let Brihaspati acknowledge my design, the son of Agniras, this (my) speech: of whom the gods, the deities, came into being let that desire, well conducting, go after us.

Sayana considers 2-4 three verses are prayer to Vak-Devata-Goddess of Speech, hence he takes Akuti as Tatparyarupa *(1/IV/1797)*. Bloomfield takes Akuti as the goddess of schemes *(3-535)*.

Book XIX, Hymn 40:

The hymn is a prayer for pardon of an error in reciting mantras or in learning and also for wisdom, strength, and life.

In the first verse, Brihaspati is invoked to mend the error or defect of mind and that of voice (speech) which enraged Saraswati the Goddess of Speech.

The second is a prayer for wisdom and strength addressed to Holy Waters. In the third the Rishi prays:

(3) 'Do not disturb our intellect, nor our consecration, nor what tapas is ours; be they propitious to us for lengthened life, let them become (our) propitious mothers.

The fourth is a prayer to Ashvins for strength full of light which"may through the darkness carry us".

Book XIX, Hymn 43:

The hymn is a prayer to various divinities for attaining the highest spiritual value. It has eight verses:

(1) Whither the men versed in Brahman go, with tapas and consecration - thither let Agni conduct me; let Agni give me intelligence. All hail to Agni.

(2) Whither, etc.

thither let Vayu conduct me; let Vayu give me vital breath. All hail to Vayu.

(3) Whither, etc.

thither let Surya conduct me; let Surya give me power of sight. All hail to Surya.

(4) Whither, etc.

thither let Chandra conduct me; let Chandra give me Manas. All hail to Chandra

(5) Whither, etc.

thither let Soma conduct me; let soma give me vital sap. All hail to Soma.

(6) Whither, etc.

thither let Indra conduct me; let Indra bestow upon me strength, All hail to Indra!

(7) Whither, etc.

thither let Waters conduct me; let immortality approach me. All hail to Waters!

(8) Whither, etc. thither let Brahma conduct me; let Brahma give Brahman unto me. All hail to Brahman

Commentary

(I) Sayana takes Brahmavid as Brahman-knowers; Dikshaya= दण्डकृष्णाजिनमेखलादि-धारणात्मिका ।He quotes the Taittiriya Brahmana as— दण्डेन दीक्षयति । मेखलया दीक्षयति । कृष्णाजिनेन दीक्षयति । *(1/IV/1931)* that is, consecrates by giving staff, girdle and black-antelope skin. (VIII) He takes Brahma as Hiranyagarbha and Brahman as lustre that comes through the Vedic learning *(1/IV/1933).*

(I) Griffith takes Brahm-vid as learned in spiritual knowledge. Diksha as cleansing rite *(6/II/299).*

Book XIX, Hyman 64:

The hymn is employed by the Kaushika-sutra in the ceremony of initiation of Vedic student to accompany the laying of four sticks of fuel on the fire *(4 (57:24-26):160) one at each verse (4:160f).*

The hymn is a prayer to Agni for long-life and various blessings. It has four verses:

(1) For lofty Jatavedas I have brought the fuel let that Jatavedas bestow faith and intelligence on me.

(2) With fuel and with flaming wood we, Jatavedas, strengthen thee; so do thou strengthen us in turn with progeny and with riches.

(3) Whatever even be the logs which Agni, we lay down for thee; propitious be that all to me; enjoy it, O most youthful god.

(4) Agni, these logs are thine, with these 0 burning one, be united, vouchsafe us (long) life-time and give the teacher immortality.

Commentary

(I) Sayana renders Medham as retention of the Vedas learnt *(1/IV/1998)*

(II) Sayana takes Idhma as flaming wood *(1/IV/1998). Griffith explains Samidh as kindling stick or firebrand with which the fire is lighted as distinct from Idhma or fuel (6/II/318).*

(IV) Sayana explains the second hemistich as "give us life (long-life) and to our teacher who initiated us, consecrated us with the Gayatri Mantra and imparted us the knowledge of Vedas, give immortality" *(1/IV/1999).* Whitney notes - The passage in the Parashara Grihya Sutra (ii,4,3), which treats of the ceremony of initiation to which these verses belong, contains in fact a prayer of the student on behalf of his initiator *(13/II/1004).*

Book XIX, Hymn 68:

The Hymn is employed at the initiation ceremony, as to be murmured prior to pronouncing the sacred 'Gayatri' *4(139.10) 297).* It is an obscure hymn and the words Avyasas and Vyasas create difficult problems for translators as well as for the commentators. Sayana takes them as Prana and Vyana and Bila as Muladhara, and Veda as the Veda *(1/IV/2002).* Whitney takes them as non-expansion and expansion *(13/II/1006-7).)* Griffith takes them as broad and narrow *(6/II/319).* Sarkar takes them as uncompiled and compiled (literature of Vedas) *(12:11-13).* Griffith takes Vedam as bunch of grass - Darbha-grass *(6/II/319).* The Hymn has only one verse:

(1) Both of broad and narrow I with magic power unclose the mouth,

With these two having taken up the Veda, we then perform rites.

COMPLETION OF THE STUDY OF THE VEDAS

Like the initiation, the end of student life ceremony had its appropriate ceremonial.

Book I, Hymn 30

The hymn is employed in the dismissal from Vedic study *(4(139.15 :297).* At the completion of his course the pupil receives blessings from the teacher for protection of the gods and long-life. The hymn is addressed to all the Gods for protection and long-life. The hymn has four verses. The second and third run as:

(2) Listen, one minded, to this utterance of mine, the sons, O Gods, among you the fathers, to you all I trust this man, happily unto old age shall ye carry him.

(3) Ye, O Gods, that are in the heaven, that are on earth, that are in the atmosphere, in the herbs, in the cattle, within the waters - do ye grant this man life to full old age, and let him escape the hundred other ways of dying.

Griffith takes it for the occasion of the consecration of a king *(6/1/34)*.

Book II, Hymn 29:

The hymn is also employed in the rite on the return home of a Vedic student *(13/I/70)*. It is a charm for obtaining long-life and prosperity etc. It has seven verses. The first runs as:

(1) Gods, give him all that earth hath best with bodily strength and happy fate; Agni and Surya grant him life, Brihaspati give him eminence.

Book XIX, Hymn 72:

The hymn is used at the end of the ceremony of commencement of Vedic study *(13/II/1009)*, also used at the time of giving dakshina *(4-310)*. According to Griffith it is a sacrificial formula *(6/II/320)*. It has only one verse. It runs as:

(1) Out of what receptacle we bore up the Veda, within that do we set it down; what is performed (and) sacrificed by the heroic might of the Brahman, with that fervour, O Gods, favour ye me here.

III. STUDENT LIFE

Book I, Hymn 33

The hymn is used in Godana ceremony to accompany bathing after shaving (of the pupil) *(1/I/159)*.

The hymn is a prayer to the waters for blessings. It has four verses. The second verse runs as:

(2) They in the midst whereof king Varuna moveth, viewing men's righteous and unrighteous dealing; they who took Agni as a germ, fair-coloured, those waters bring felicity and bless us!

Book I, Hymn 34:

The hymn is a charm to get victory in debates *(1/I/.162)*. It has five verses. The second runs as:

(2) My tongue hath honey at the tip, and sweetest honey at the root; Thou yieldest to my wish and will, and shall be mine and only mine.

Whitney and Griffith take it as a love-spell *(13/I/34, 6/I/38)*.

Book III, Hymn 30:

Sayana regards the hymn as included under the designation Ganakarmani and so it is used in the Upakarman *(1/I/393). According to Griffith the hymn is a prayer to secure love and concord in a family (6/I/125)*. "In the Kaushika- Sutra 12-5 this hymn heads a gana or series of seven Atharvan charms which are designated as Sammanasyani - designed to prdouce harmony" *(3:361-62)*. The Atharvan abounds in such songs of harmony. The hymn has seven verses. The sixth runs as:

(6) Identical shall be your drink, in common shall be your share of food! I yoke you together in the same traces : do ye worship Agni, joining together, as spokes around about the hub!

Book VI, Hymn 1:

Sayana enjoins that the hymn is to be used to consecrate a dish which is to be eaten after the Samavartana *(1/II/639)*. In Whitney's view it is a prayer in praise of Savitar. It is used with others to win wealth by Vedic knowledge *(13/I/281-82)*. The hymn has three verses. The third runs as:

(3) May he, indeed, God Savitar, impel for us many Amritas, both the good praises, unto welfare.

Book VI, Hymn 64:

This hymn is also rubricated in the series, entitled Sammanasyani in the Kaushika-Sutra 12, 5. It is a hymn for concord. It has three verses. The first runs as:

(1) Do ye agree, unite yourself, may your minds be in harmony, just as the Gods of Old in harmony sat down to their share.

Book VI, Hymn 94:

This too belongs to the series entitled Sammanasyani. It is also a hymn for concord.

Book VII, Hymn 12

The hymn is a prayer for influence at deliberative and religious meetings. Sayana employs this in the rite of initiation (reciting this ghee is offered) *(1/II/891)*. The hymn is rubricated in the series Sabhajaya Karmani. The hymns are used in the performances which procure victory in the assembly etc. The hymn has four verses. The third runs as:

(3) Of these men seated here I make the splendour and the lore mine own. Indra, make me conspicuous in all this gathered company.

Book VII, Hymn 16:

The hymn is employed to waken the pupil, found asleep after sunrise *(1/II/896)*. Griffith takes it as a prayer for prosperity and notes that it is employed in the ritual to wake the sleeping priest *(6/I/335f)*. It has only one verse. It runs as:

(1) O Brihaspati, Savitar, increase thou him; enlighten him unto great good-fortune; sharpen him thoroughly though already sharpened : Let all the Gods revel after him.

Book VII, Hymn 105:

The hymn is used in the initiation as the teacher takes the pupil by the arm and sets him facing eastward; and the second half verse later in the same, as he makes him (the pupil) turn so as to face him *(4(55:16, 154-55)*. Griffith takes it as an initiation formula and notes that the stanza is spoken by the Acharya in the Upanayana ceremony, when he invests the religious student with the sacrificial thread, instructs him in the Veda, and gives him authority to teach *(6/I/379)*. The hymn has one verse. It runs as:

(1) Leaving humanity behind, making the heavenly word the choice, with all thy companions, turn thou unto guidances.

Book XIX, Hymn 71:

The hymn is a prayer addressed to Veda-mother (Gayatri) for various blessings. Sayana enjoins its use in the worship of the Veda that one has studied, or of the Gayatri *(I/IV/2004)*. It has only one verse. It runs as:

(1) Praised by me (is) the boon-bestowing Veda-mother. Let them further the twice-born's song that honours Soma. Go ye to Brahma's world having enriched me with life and breath, with children and with cattle, with fame and wealth and with Vedic splendour.

Sayana takes Maya as muttering the sacred Gayatri through the Vedic study and Pavamani as purifying *(1/IV/2005)*. Whitney and Griffith take Pavamani as Soma-hymn *(13/II/1008, 6/II/320)*. Griffith takes Veda-mata as libations *(6/II/320)*.

FINDINGS

In the RV*, there is no explicit reference to the ceremony of initiation which received great importance in the later ages. The home of the teacher was the school where his son received lessons along with a few neighbouring students. The word Brahmacharin in the technical sense of a religious student is found in the RV *(10:X,109,5)*. Sharpening of intellect and cultivation of moral character in the Brahmacharin were the aims of educational system. This is evident from the celebrated Gayatri Mantra *(10:III,62,10)*. The fundamental educational method was tapas and austerity as a process of self-realization *(9/I/104-105)*.

With the development and elaboration of the institution of the Yajna and the growth of a vast literature relating to it, the problem of the preservation of this literature became acute. In the age of the later Samhitas the whole of the Vedic literature was looked upon as Shruti; so it must therefore have formed the chief subject of instruction and vital part of education. Evidently, then, the method of teaching the sacred hymnology and sacrificial ritual must have become more and more systematized during this age. Literary education was transmitted by word of mouth from teacher to pupil an echo of which is found in the frog-hymn of the RV.

THE INITIATION IN THE AV

There is a specific mention of the investiture of intiation in the third verse of the famous hymn (5) of the eleventh book - extolling the Vedic student.

आचार्यो उपनयमानो ब्रह्मचारिणं कृणुते गर्भमन्तः ।

तं रात्रीस्तिस्त्र उदरे बिभर्ति तं जातं द्रष्टुमभिसंयन्ति देवाः ।।

From here*, the following abbreviations may be taken into account :

AV = Atharva-veda
RV = Rigveda
Kau. = Kaushika-Sutra

The hymn gives many details of the Upanayana Samskara found in the later day ceremonies. The Vedic student was called Brahmacharin and the teacher Acharya. The teacher performs for the pupil the part of a spiritual mother; and by the initiation ceremony the youth is born anew. The teacher receives the Brahmachari as a disciple, he places him as an embryo within; he bears him in his belly for three nights; when he is born the Gods convene to see him. In the AV the word उपनयन is used in the sense of "taking charge of a student". That is initiation of the child by a teacher into sacred lore. The Shatapatha Brahmana states, "By laying his right hand on (the pupil), the teacher becomes pregnant (with him); in the third (night) he is born as a Brahmana with the Savitri" *(5/XLIV-5/ii,5,4,12)*. Even in the Sutra period the proposal of the student for studentship and its acceptance by the teacher is the central point in the investiture *(11:115)*. Apastamba says "He (Acharya) regenerates him (the pupil) from out of knowledge. That is the highest life. The parents create only the body."[1] The pupil owes his spiritual life to the teacher, hence he should always be revered.

The pupil wore sacred girdle, put on the antelope-skin, kept long beard, practised austerity, collected fuel and offered them in the sacred fire. He also begged alms. All these characteristics of a student referred to in the verses 4, 6 and 9 of the hymn re-appear in the post-Vedic literature on the ritual. So Raj Bali Pandey concluded that, "It may be argued that during the Atharvavedic times the Upanayana was regarded as a second birth and, most probably all the twice-born received their status from this rite" *(11:122)*.

In the beginning the Upanayana ceremony was very simple. The student approached his teacher with sacrificial fuel in his hands, thereby showing that he intended to be his pupil and that he was ready to serve the teacher. According to Raj Bali Pandey, "Even before the close of the Vedic period, the ceremony was assuming a complicated character. The Upanayana of the Atharvavedic time included many items of the later- day ritual" *(11:127)*.

---

1 Infra:18

CEREMONIES FOR ADMISSION INTO VEDIC STUDENTSHIP

I. Shaving (Book VI, Hymn 68)

The hymn is employed in the Upanayana at the beginning of the whole ceremony to accompany the act of shaving. It might be connected with the Diksha.

II. Godana (Book I, Hymn 33)

The hymn is used in Godana ceremony to accompany bathing after shaving. This Samskara (shaving and bath) was called Godana as it was characterized by the gift of a cow to the teacher and gifts to the barber.

III. The Girdle (Book VII, Hymn 67(69))

The hymn is employed in the Upanayana, in the reception of girdle.

(ii) The Acharya ties round the waist of the youth the girdle duly consecrated with the hymn (VI-133). The teacher binds the girdle round the pupil to protet his purity and chastity and to keep him away from evil.

IV. The Sacred Thread (Book VII, Hymn 105)

The hymn is used in the initiation as the teacher takes the pupil by the arm and sets him facing eastward; and the second half verse later in the same, as he makes him turn so as to face him. It is an initiation formula and the verse is spoken by the Acharya, when he invests the pupil with the sacred thread, instructs him in the Veda, and gives him authority to teach.

V. Krishnajina (Book XI, Hymn 5, Verse VI)

The black-antelope skin is prescribed for the Brahmacharin. It is one of the symbols of Brahmanical worship and civilization. When the deerskin became connected with the religious ceremony, the writers on Dharma invested it with symbolism.

Here it symbolizes holy lustre and intellectual and spiritual pre-eminence *(8:24)*. "The student, while putting it on, was reminded that he should attain the spiritual and intellectual position of a Rishi" *(11:134)*.

VI. The Staff (Book VI, Hymn 48)

The hymn is employed in the initiation for delivering a staff to a Vedic student. The teacher gives the staff to the pupil and he accepts it for the sake of long life, of holy lustre and holiness. The staff was the symbol of a traveller and while accepting it, the student prayed that he may reach safely the end of his long and arduous journey *(2:25,26)*. The staff could also serve the purpose of making the student self-confident and self-reliant, when he went out in the forest for collecting fuel, for tending the cattle of his teacher or when he travelled in darkness *(11:134.35)*. In this sense it may be taken up with the VI-40 -- a prayer for freedom from fear *(12:16)* and also with the VI-56 which is designed to keep serpents away.

VII. Taking the Charge (Book I, Hymn 9)

The hymn is uttered by the teacher at the initiation ceremony for the formal acceptance of the pupil. Here the teacher entrusts the earthly as well as the heavenly success of the pupil to the care of deities like Agni, Varuna, Indra, Adityas etc.

VIII. The Savitri Mantra

(i) (Book XIX, Hymn 68)

The hymn is employed at the Upanayana, as to be murmured prior to pronouncing the sacred Gayatri.

(ii) (Book XIX, Hymn 71)

The hymn is a prayer addressed to Veda-mother-- Gayatri.

The teaching of the Gayatri-mantra signalizes the second birth of the child. He is born as a Brahmana with the Savitri. The Sun and the Goddess Savitri are worshipped to stimulate and develop talent.

IX. The Sacred Fire (Book XIX, Hymn 64)

The rite of first enkindling and feeding of the sacred fire is performed after the teaching of Gayatri. The hymn is employed in the Upanayana to accompany the laying of four sticks of fuel on the fire, one at each verse. The verses are full of educational significance. The sacred fire is the symbol of life and light for the pupil. The pupil prays for Shraddha, Medha, Offspring, riches, bliss and long-life and concludes his prayer thus "O Agni, give the teacher immortality".

X. The Rounds for Alms (Book VI, Hymn 71)

The hymn is employed in a rite for obviating ill effects from acceptance of gifts and in the Upanayana, accompanying an offering by the pupil from the food obtained by begging. The begging Brahmachari offers, while reciting the hymn, the fruits of his mendicancy. Whatever gift he brought through begging he wants that to be purified hence he prays "May Agni the priest, render that an auspicious offering".

XI. Rishihastaka (Book I, Hymn 9; Book VIII; Hymn 1, 2)

These hymns are employed in the course of investiture of initiation in certain special ceremonies -- Rishihastaka -- calculated to ensure longevity. The hymns are recited by the teacher by touching the pupil's navel.

(Book IV, Hymn 13)

The hymn is employed in the ceremonies for long-life that follows the initiation. This also comes under the rubric Rishihastaka. While reciting sixth and seventh verse of the hymn the seer touches the pupil for his well-being.

XII. (Book VII, Hymns 32, 33, 53)

The hymns belong to Ayushya Gana that is prayers for long-life. The hymns are very uniform in character and are generally employed in the Upanayana to ensure long life.

(Book IV, Hymns 9 and 10)

Both the hymns are employed in connection with a practice for bestowing long-life and prospertiy upon the young disciple after the investiture. (i) While reciting IV-9 an amulet of salve is fastened upon the pupil, (ii) While reciting IV-10 an amulet of pearl is fastened upon the pupil.

XIII. (Book VI, Hymns 38, 58)

The hymns belong to Varchasya Ganas. The object of both the hymns and the practices connected with it is to endow (a king, here) a pupil with varchas and more particularly to transfer to him the Varchas inherent in Snataka, animals and brilliant substances (38). The fifty eighth is a prayer for glory and power, it appears with various others with an oblation to Agni in the Upanayana. Both are employed in the Utsarjana rite — rite of dedication performed on entering upon Vedic study.

The teacher wants his pupil to be active, firmly built and strong because it is only for such youth the earth becomes full of wealth.

XIV. Medhajanana (Book I, Hymn 1; VI, 69, 108; VII, 61; XIX, 4)

After the initiation ceremonies were over the pupil was required to observe three days' continence which was termed as Triratra Vrata *(11:139)*. At the end of the vow, the Medhajanana ritual was performed in order to get divine help in the stimulation of intellect and retaining power. The ceremony speaks of high concern of the teacher about the intellectual well-being of the pupil.

The hymns are employed in the Medhajanana ceremony. The hymn (Bk. I, 1) is a prayer addressed to Vachaspati - the Lord of Speech for divine help, favour and illumination. The hymn (Bk. VII.61) is a prayer for success in penance and for the acquisition of sacred knowledge and its fruits. The hymn (Bk. XIX.4) is a prayer for the attainment of a wish.

The hymn (Bk.VI.108) is explicitly a prayer for wisdom. The pupil through this prayer wants to get bliss of that 'Intelligence which is lauded by sages, sped by prayers, trusted by Brahmacharin and which the creative Rishis and men endowed with wisdom know'. He wants such Intelligence day and night so he plants in him Intelligence by his prayers -- " मेधां वचसा आवेशया महे"

XV. Parishajjay or Sabhajaya

(i) Book i, 34; IV, 1; VII, 12)

The hymns are charms for influence at deliberative and religious meetings, they too are employed in the rite of initiation.

(ii) Book III, 8)

The hymn is a prayer for authority and is employed in the initiation.

The pupil here prays for authority -- to get centre position in his group.

The pupil wishes to achieve his two wishes that is to win the contest and to be midmost in his group with divine grace but not at the cost of the decent corporate life hence he wants to win them on merit and with the consentient of his fellow students.

XVI. Prayer to secure harmony (Book III, 30; VI, 64,94).

For the smooth progress of educational process there must be a complete harmony between the teacher and his disciples and there must be a bond of harmonious relation between the students. The three hymns belong to a Gana designated as Sammanasyani -- designed to produce harmony. The hymns are prayers to promote harmony, love and unanimity in the corporate life of the ashrama.

XVII. Other Symbolical Performance

(i) Book VI, Hymn 53)

The hymn is applied in the Upanayana. While reciting VI, 53, 3 along with others the water bowl is consecrated in which the pupil sees his face. The significance of the rite is not clear and Raj Bali Pandey did not mention it in the Upanayana.

(ii) (Book VII, Hymn 54((56,57(i))

The hymn is employed in the initiation as one looks at the Sun and asks his protection for the pupil. The hymn is addressed to Indra. On the basis of its contents Griffith's view that the hymn is a charm to obtain knowledge of the Veda appears reasonable.

End of Studentship (Book I, 30; II,29; VI,1; XIX,72)

The end of student life ceremony is termed as Samavartana which means 'returning home from the house of the teacher'.

(i) These hymns are employed in the rite on the return home of a Vedic student. The hymn (Bk. I, 30) is recited by the teacher at the completion of his pupil's course to bless him with long-life and to secure for him divine protection. (ii) The hymn (Bk. II, 29) is a charm for obtaining long-life and prosperity. (iii) The hymn (Bk. VI, 1) is employed to consecrate a dish which is to be eaten after the Samavartana. And the hymn (B. XIX, 72) is employed in the Samavartana ceremony at the time of giving dakshina to the teacher.

CONCLUSION

From the foregoing discussion of the hymns selected for the study it becomes quite clear that during the Atharvavedic times 'upa-ni' was already a technical term for "receive as pupil, initiate". The ceremony of initiation is first adumbrated in the AV, by which the teacher initiates the pupil into new life termed as second birth whence he becomes a dvija - twice-born. By the initiation the teacher regenerates the pupil from out of knowledge. That is the highest life. The parents create only the body. The famous hymn (XI;5) in glory of the Brahmahari gives many details of the Upanayana Samskara found in the later day ceremonies.

The aims of education are stated to be faith, steadfast- wisdom, progeny, wealth, longevity and immortality (XIX,64). The aim thus comprehended both material and spiritual excellence. Rishihood endowed with creative fervour was their ideal (VI:133). The Vedic educators wanted their pupils to be active, firmly built, strong, sagacious, moral, austere and devout. The way to achieve these excellences was penance, austerity, consecration and continence. ब्रह्मचर्य, दीक्षा and तपस् were considered basic to all prosperity material, moral, spiritual. They prayed to the divinities to lead them to the abode -- "whither the men versed in Brahman go with tapas and consecration".

The teacher was considered to be a spiritual mother of the disciple. Brahmacharya, holy vows, self-restraint and purity were regarded pre-eminent virtues. It is by these qualities that the teacher finds the pupil. The teacher regulates the life of pupil like Yama but he is also propitious like Varuna and delightful like the Moon. He is diligent in his penance and holy vows. The Vedic educator seems to be very much concerned in the well-being and prosperity of his pupil.

The new life of Brahmacharin has its own discipline and vows for the pupil. He is clad in the black-antelope skin, wears girdle of Kusa grass and lets his hair grow long. He has also to collect fuel to offer both morning and evening to the sacrificial fire by which he himself becomes illuminated. Begging is also one of his duties, but he lives on the gifts of the pious. He is to be diligent in his study of the Vedas and in his penance. His is a life consecrated by vows and illuminated by tapas. He fills the teacher by his tapas. He is graphically drawn as stood in the water kindled with tapas and when he has bathed in the ocean, shines exceedingly upon earth, brown and ruddy.

The following items were found included in the Upanayana ceremony (1) Shaving with Godana; (2) Giving of the Girdle, Sacred Thread, Krishnajin and Staff; (3) Taking the charge;(4) Teaching of Savitri Mantra; (5) Enkindling and feeding of the Sacred Fire; (6) Rounds for Alms; (7) Rites for conferring Varchas, long-life etc.; (8) Medhajanana and (9) Rites for harmony and getting victory in the contest.

In the end of student life ceremony the following items were found included (1) Teacher's blessings; (2) Eating of dish after Samavartana; (3) Giving dakshina.

There are prescriptions as to the time of study or refraining from study of the sacred texts-- in cloudy weather, in sight of green barley, within hearing of cattle. There are also prayers for supplying lost or destroyed staff, laying pieces of fuel in renewing a lost fire, and for pardon of an error in reciting mantras or in learning. There is also a hymn employed to waken a pupil (found asleep after sunrise).

REFERENCES

Original Sources

(1) Vishva Bandhu. *Atharvaveda (Shaunaka) The Pada-Patha and SayanaCharya's Commentary*. Hoshiyarpur: Vishveshvarananda Vedic Research Institute, Part I, 1960, Parts II and III, 1961, Parts II and III, 1961, Part IV(I), 1962.

Secondary Sources

(2) A.S. Altekar. *Education in Ancient India*. Benares : The Indian Book Shop, 1934.

(3) Maurice Bloomfield. *Hymns of The Atharva-Veda*. Delhi : Motilal Banarsidass, 1964.

(4) ———— (ed.). *The Kaushika Sutra Of Atharva Veda*. Delhi : Motilal Banarsidass, 1972.

(5) Julius Eggeling. *Shatapatha - Brahmana*. London : Oxford, 1900.

(6) Ralph T.H. Griffith. *Hymns Of The Atharvaveda Translated with a Popular Commentary*. Varanasi : Chowkhamba, Vols. I, II, 1961.

(7) R.C. Majumdar. *The Vedic Age*. London : George Allen and Unwin Ltd., 1951.

(8) R.L. Mitra (ed.). *Gopatha Brahmana* (Of Atharvaveda). Delhi : Indological Book House, 1972.

(9) R.K. Mookerji. *Hindu Civilization. Part I.* Bombay : Bharatiya Vidya Bhavan, 1957.

(10) F. Max Muller (ed.). *Rigveda Samhita*. London : Oxford Unviersity, 1890-2.

(11) R.B. Pandey. *Hindu Samskaras*. Delhi : Motilal Banarasidass, 1969.

(12) S.C. Sarkar. *Educational Ideas and Instiuttions in Ancient India*. Patna : Janaki Prakashan, 1979.

(13) William Dwight Whitney. *Atharva Veda Samhita – Translated with a Critical and Exegetical Commentary*. Delhi : Motilal Banarasidass, Vols. I, II, 1962.

[illegible]

REFERENCES

Original Sources

[illegible]

Secondary Sources

[illegible]

[illegible]

[illegible]

[illegible]

[illegible]

[illegible]

[illegible]

[illegible]

[illegible]

[illegible]

[illegible]

[illegible]

EDUCATION IN THE VISHNU PURANA

The importance of Puranic works has been widely recognised by scholars for the study of the social, religious and political history of ancient India. The need has already been keenly felt to study these works for valuable information about the constitution of its people, about the ideas and beliefs of the various tribes living in its different parts, and also about its geography, literature, mythology, ideas and superstitions, flora and fauna and so on.

The principal Puranas are eighteen in number and they are classified as Brahma, Vaishnav and Shaiva. They deal with the various aspects of the Trinity - Brahma, Vishnu and Shiva and their consorts. The term Purana implies 'old' whch indicates the object of the compilation to be the preservation of ancient traditions. According to Wilson the lexicon of Amara Sinha gives as a synonym of Purana, Pancha- Lakshanam, 'that which has five characteristic topics' *(4:iv)*. The oft quoted definition of a Purana is also found in the Vishnu Purana *(4/VI/8:2,13)*.

सर्गश्च प्रतिसर्गश्च वंशो मन्वन्तराणि च।
वंशानुचरितं चैव पुराणं पञ्चलक्षणम्।।

The ideal Purana deals with (1) Primary creation, (2) Secondary creation, (3) Genealogy of gods and patriarchs, (4) The reigns and periods of Manus, and (5) The history of the two great races of kings, the solar and the lunar. The Vishnu Purana is considered to be the best specimen of these traditional five characteristics *(4:(b))*. The Purana is divided into six books and they contain 126 chapters. The Vishnu Purana is written in generally correct and, easy-flowing and elegant Sanskrit and has the character of a unified work *(4:(c))*. It is an authentic work from the point of view of both religion and society.

The present study of the Vishnu Purana was undertaken with a view (1) to locating the episodes of the Purana having educational implications and to interpreting them, (2) to collecting and coordinating the other material of the Purana having educational implications and to presenting it all in an organized form.

Method

The main source of the data was the Original Sanskrit Text of the *Vishnu Purana,* published by The Geeta Press, Gorakhpur (third edition). For English rendering of the text, the author has freely drawn from the *English Translation of the Vishnu Purana* by H.H. Wilson without disturbing the original meaning.

The Vedic Age, The Age of Imperial Unity and *The Classicial Age,* the works on History and Culture of the Indian People published by Bharatiya Vidya Bhavan were also consulted.

The material has been discussed under the following heads:

I. The episodes having educational implications with their interpretations -

(i) The Prahlada Episode

(ii)The Ribhu and Nidagha Episode

(iii)The Keshidhvaja and Khandikya Episode

II. The other material under the following heads -

(i) Commencing discourse (between Parashara and Maitreya)

(ii) The spirit of a nation

(iii) Concept of man

(iv) End and Means

(v) Para and Apara Vidya

(vi) Brahmacharya

(vii) Duties and Qualities of a Guru

(viii) Subjects of Study

(ix) Svadhyaya and Yoga

(x) Epistemology

(xi) Self Culture - (a) General Essential Moral-Merits

(b) Sadachara

The Prahlada Episode

The Prahlada episode is interesting and instructive. Prahlada was righteous, an inexhaustible mine of purity and truth - he was, in fact, an unfailing model for all pious men *(4/I/15:157)*. He was a devotee of the highest order who looked upon the world with mind undisturbed, and full of benignity and regarded all things with equal affection, and as identical with himself. It was his thesis that equanimity is the sole way to attain Vishnu. The best way to realize God is to identify ourselves with all things. To realize unity of Atman in all created things is equanimity -- an essential master quality to realize Vishnu *(4/I/17:90)*. In a way this rather is the thesis of the Vishnu Purana - he who is always desirous of the welfare of creatures as he is anxious about the welfare of himself and his children, attains Vishnu with ease *(4/III/8:17)*. When a person refrains from casting his evil eye on all created things, all quarters bring bliss to him *(4/IV/10:25)*. Prahlada was established in equanimity and hence he remained unscathed even in the tormenting punishment which was inflicted by his demon father.

At the proper age Prahlada was initiated and he resided in the dwellings of his preceptor, where, assiduous in attendance on his preceptor, he constantly improved in his studies. But whenever on occasions his demon father asked him as to what he derived from his studies he always truthfully replied that, "The substance of all I have learned is - Man should adore Him who is without beginning, middle or end, increase or diminution, the imperishable Lord of the world, the universal causes" *(4/I/17:14-15)*. He repeatedly told his sire that he had been very well instructed in various branches of study by his venerable teachers but he could not all in all approve them. In his opinion, "Let the person who covets the goods of fortune be meritorious and let the person who hopes for final liberation cultivate the virtue of equanimity" *(4/I/19:46)*. Even his teachers told him that as he was born in the celebrated family of Brahma, and as he was the son of the king of the demons then why he should acknowlege dependence upon gods and upon the eternal. "Your father is the stay of all worlds, as you yourself in turn shall be. Desist then from celebrating the praises of an enemy, and remember that of all venerable preceptors, a father is most venerable" *(4/I/18:11-13)*. Prahlada replied that he too admitted that he was born in the celebrated family of Marichi. He also accepted the dictum that 'father is the most venerable of holy teachers'. These advices found a ready assent in his mind but to the question as to why he should depend upon the eternal he decisively replied, "Who can give assent to this as right? The words are void of meaning". In his view the eternal Shri Hari is "the root of all riches, dignity, renown, wisdom, progeny, righteousness and liberation". If so then how can it be said, "What need is there of the eternal?"

Thus spoken by Prahlada, his teachers were incensed and had recourse to magic incantation by which a female deity of destruction was enwreathed with fire flame. She approached Prahlada and smote him with a fiery trident on the breast. The weapon fell broken into a hundred pieces upon the ground, the very magic being then turned upon the sinful priests. But Prahlada seeing them perish, appealed to Vishnu for succour. He said, "If I have been always friendly to them who have inflicted wounds upon me, then I implore you, let these, the priests be now restored to life". The teachers then rose up and ultimately blessed Prahlada *(4/I/18:33-45)*.

Prahlada was an unfailing model for all pious persons. He was a diligent student and was always assiduous in attendance to his preceptors, not only that he also respected the dictum 'father is the most venerable of holy teachers'. Despite his approval of these principles, he defied the authority of his teachers and father and disobeyed them and stood by his conviction that 'man should adore Vishnu who is the root of all prosperity, wisdom, righteousness and liberation'.

Educationally the episode poses two knotty problems -- one is academic and the other is ethical. The teachers of Prahlada and his father believed in the method of education by imposition, authority and indoctrination. The teachers wanted to indoctrinate Prahlada in the principles of civil polity prescribed by Shukra, the preceptor of the Asuras. On the other hand Prahlada firmly believed in the method of free inquiry. He repeatedly told his father that his teachers very well instructed him in various branches of study including the polity of Shukra. But he could not all in all approve them. On his own deliberation he came to the conclusion that 'Let the person who covets the goods of fortune be meritorious and let the person who hopes for final liberation cultivate the virtue of equanimity'. For his father and teacher the infinitive 'to teach' meant to settle thought but to Prahlada it meant to provoke it. His father and teacher were dedicated to heretical doctrines while Prahlada was dedicated to truth. So it was a conflict between two faiths or to put it in the modern phraseology it was an issue of academic freedom. How did we conceive of the verb 'to teach'? Did it mean to settle thought or to provoke it? Is this freedom of making interpretations proper concern for the students as well as teachers? *(2:277).*

The teacher must negotiate many personal relationships with his students, colleagues and parents in which conflicts of interest arise. Evidently the interests of the pupil and the teacher overlap and interpenetrate in a number of situations. How is the teacher to unravel and sort out these interests to ensure a judgement about them that is just and fair? This is clearly an ethical problem *(2:297).* Does the relation of pupil and teacher pose unique problems? If so, that is if it is a unique relationship then it comes under the rubric of professional ethics.

Education in ancient India had its own rituals and ceremonies to emphasize its religious aim and character as an aid to self-fulfilment and educing of personality. Education was a process of life. The very tenor of life was changed for the pupil who had to leave the home of his parents to live in a new home, the home of his spiritual parent *(6/II--:582).*

The teacher was the central figure, the very pivot of the educational system with which the State had very little to do. He would introduce the child to studentship, and was in sole charge of his moral, mental and physical upbringing. The relationship between the teacher and pupil was in no sense mercenary, but sacred and almost spiritual. The teacher was friend, philosopher and guide to the pupil. The initiation of the boy into studentship by the teacher marked, as it were, his second birth *(5/I/517).*

The teacher occupies a very exalted position in ancient India. He was an object of worship *(I:1).* According to Lokamanya Tilak the teachers were renowned not for opulence and mundane prosperity but for their wisdom, integrity and dedication to duty. Rishihood was their ideal. The Rishis were untouched by avarice and free from wordly desires. They had subdued their passions. They were endowed with goodness, wisdom and tranquility. It was due to these qualities that they commanded the honour of the people. In their hermitages the knotty problems like, where lies the strength of Swadharma, how could the corporate life of the society be maintained and sustained, what is doable and what is not, what are the duties of the king and that of the people, how the people should act when a king deviates from his duties and what the king should do when the people transgress the path of duty, etc., were independently deliberated with utmost patience, dispassionateness and disinterestedness. It was obvious that such ashramas had provided brilliant and dignified students with dynamic character having implicit faith in their teachers that when asked for a solution of a knotty problem they would give only the true and rightful answer. They knew that their teachers were dedicated to truth only and had no fear in telling it either of a monarch or of the populace *(9/II/557-58)*. The teacher's obligation is to truth. He must be free from an influence that prevents him from stating the truth. His watchword should be 'know the truth and practise the truth'. Truth is grounded in the nature of things, so is the right to search for it. Teaching must lead to independent thinking and free investigation. 'To teach' means to cause the child to deliberate, to ponder. The teacher should not impose anything or insist upon anything but leave his students to weigh the matters critically. The students must be free to accept or reject the matter taught. They must be free to make their own judgements.

Jamnalal Bayti stated that the teacher in ancient India was not supposed to impose anything upon his pupils but was developing in the taught the ability to think rationally. Before accepting anything, the students got ample chances to think, to listen rationally on all issues *(I:2)*.

But this was not the case with the teachers of Prahlada. They were not motivated with the sublime ideal of teachership but were impelled by selfish interest -- to receive favours from the demon king Hiranya Kashyapu and were very much afraid of his wrath. It was under these pressures that they were asserting their authority and were punishing the right conduct of Prahlada. Ultimately Prahlada had to defy them.

When the college heads tried to check the right spirit of students -- their ready response to the boycott movement in the agitation against the vivisection of Bengal *(1905)*, Tilak wrote three articles denouncing the college authorities and declared that "These surely are not our Gurus". In his opinion the teacher must be free from any influence that prevents him from stating truth and he must be bold enough to act accordingly. Being an educator of the highest order Tilak was very much conscious of the delicate relationship between the teacher and the student but he maintained that teachers or elderly persons in the house should not assert their authority in a wrong manner and punish the right conduct of people as indiscipline *(9/II/399)*.

It is here that Tilak quoted the example of Prahlada who defied his sire and teachers for his right convictions. Tilak equated the college authorities who punished the right spirit of the students with the teachers of Prahlada, who were appointd by the demon king to indoctrinate Prahlada in their principles. Both were motivated by selfish interest -- to bask under the sunshine of royal favours, and both were very much afraid of the royal wrath *(10/III/238)*.

On the authority of Mahabharata and Prahlada episode Tilak mainained that when a teacher, who is motivated by selfish interests, or is under the thumb of others or has lost the poise of his intellect -- when such a teacher without knowing the desirability or undesirability of action, orders his pupil or punishes his pupil for not obeying his command, the pupil is perforce to defy the teacher *(10/III/238, 242, 243, 248)*.

When there is a conflict between the right motivation of the student and asserting of authority of the teacher in a wrong manner the student has to disobey his teacher following the Prahlada-Vritti. The moral power of assertion of the right and the courage to defy the wrong is termed as Prahlda- Vritti in Tilak's philosophy. The very spirit of Prahlada- Vritti came to be known as Satyagraha in the Gandhian era.

Episode of Ribhu and Nidagha

The episode of Ribhu ad Nidagha is a graphic narration of how a teacher brings desirable change in the pupil. The teacher's method was practical and was capable of bringing desirable change in the pupil.

The teacher was Ribhu the son of Brahma and the disciple was Nidagha who was the son of seer Pulastya. Ribhu felt that even after receiving the knowledge of all sciences his disciple Nidagha did not establish himself in the doctrine of unity. So Ribhu went to Veernagar the beautiful abode of Nidagha. Nidagha respectfully received him. When he washed his hands and feet Nidagha requested him to eat. On this Ribhu told Nidagha that he was not fond of despised viands and asked for rice boiled with sugar, wheaten cakes and milk with curd and molasses. Nidagha's wife served the desired food to Ribhu and when he had dined well Nidagha humbly asked him whether he had eaten sufficiently and with pleasure and also inquired, "Where is your present residence? Whether do you propose to go? whence, holy sir, have you now come?" To this Ribhu replied, "Hunger and thirst are the functions of the body. Pleasure and contentment are the faculties of mind. They are in no way related to the Atman. The Atman being all-pervading, your questions regarding residence etc. are useless". To the inquiry as to why Ribhu made distinction between sweet and unsweet food, Ribhu stated that sweet or unsweet both were relative terms and "that which is sweet is no longer so when it occasions the sense of repletion; and that which is not sweet becomes sweet when a man (being very hungry) fancies that it is so". So the mind which properly judges of what is or is not sweet is impressed with the notion of identity, and that this effect of identity tends to liberation *(4/II/15:3-31)*.

Hearing the sublime truth from Ribhu, Nidagha said, "Who are y ou, oh sir, who came here for my welfare?" Ribhu replied, "My son, I am your teacher, came here to communicate to you true wisdom. Know this whole universe as the form of divine". Thus having spoken and receiving homage of Nidagha, Ribhu went his way *(4/II/15:32-36)*.

After the expiry of another one thousand years, Ribhu again came to Nidagha to instruct him in true wisdom. When he arrived near the town (where Nidagha dwelt), Ribhu beheld a prince entering into it, with a retinue; and his pupil Nidagha standing afar off, avoiding the crowd. Ribhu approached him and saluting him demanded why he was standing in such a retired spot. Nidagha replied, "There is a great crowd of people attending the entrance of the king into the town, and I am staying here to avoid it". "Tell me, excellent Brahman", said Ribhu, "for I believe that you are wise, which is here the king and which is any other man?" Nidagha answered that the person who was seated on the stately elephant was the king and others were his attendants. Ribhu observed, "You have shown me at one moment the elephant, and the king, without noticing any peculiar characteristic by which they may be distinguished. Tell me, venerable sir, is there any difference between them? For I am desirous to know which is here the elephant, which is the king?" "The elephant", answered Nidagha, "is underneath; the king is above him. Who is not aware, Brahman, of the relation between that which bears and that which is borne?" To this Ribhu rejoined, "Still explain to me, according to what I know of it, this matter, what is meant by the word underneath, and what is it that is termed above?" As soon as he had uttered this Nidagha jumped upon Ribhu and said, "Here is my answer: I am above like the Raja and you are underneath, like the elephant". "Very well", said Ribhu, "you, it seems, are as it were the Raja, and I am like the elephant; but come now do you tell me which of us two is you; which is I". When Nidagha heard these words, he immediately fell at the feet of the stranger, and said, "Surely, you are my saintly preceptor Ribhu; the mind of no other person is so fully established in the doctrine of unity as that of my teacher, and hence I know that you are he". Ribhu said, "Oh Nidagha, I am indeed your preceptor Ribhu whom you served with fullest attention and reverence, hence my love for you brought me here to instruct you. Oh magnanimous, I had instructed you in brief the essence of sublime truth -- which is the non-duality of all". Having thus spoken to Nidagha, Ribhu went away, leaving his disciple profoundly impressed, by his instruction, with belief in unity. Nidagha beheld all beings thenceforth as the same with himself, and, perfect in holy knowledge, obtained final liberation *(4/II/16:1-20)*.

In ancient India education was treated as a process of growth. Education is the facilitation of the growth of the child as it unfolds the essentials of its self. In a technical sense Vidya refers to that knowledge of Brahman and its oneness with the individual selves, which leads the aspirant to the attainment of the highest that is possible to him *(3:299)*.

Commenting on the first verse of the Kena Upanishad, Shankar stated that "There are statements made by both in the Shrutis and Smritis like: 'He who has a preceptor knows; the knowledge obtained through a preceptor alone yields the best result' "*(3:173)*. Commenting on the same verse Vallabha stated that association with saints is necessary to comprehend the essential nature of Brahman, for Brahman can be realised only by reflection with pure mind. Reflection requires intelligence with firm conviction consequent upon the final solution of all doubts about allied subjects. The saints here are Acharyas who abide in Brahman and who are well-versed in the Shruti. The scriptures state -- 'In order to know Him, one must approach with sacrificial sticks- Samidha in hand, the master, abiding in Brahman and well- versed in the Vedas'*(3:177)*. The truth cannot be comprehended if taught by an ordinary man but it can be easily known if taught by another who is superior.

The aim of education is self-realization; knowledge is the continous awareness of the self in the process of realization; ignorance is unawareness of a soul unrealized; the teacher is a guide, a model, a friend, to stimulate and inspire the continuous process of realization. Ribhu was the teacher of this ideal type. The attentive services rendered to him by his disciple Nidagha so overwhelmed him that he continuously thought of his disciple's final welfare. His two meetings with his pupil turned out to be the best educative occasions for dissolving the dualism into a harmony, unity and wholeness of the inner and the outer. Educative process must gradually lead to an inner awakening and knowledge of the self and the relation of the self to things and their relations; and that finally leads to the knowledge of God as the fountain source of one's life, as the cause and unity of all things from whose eternal spirit all reality proceeds and upon whom it all depends and in whom it all rests.

The Keshidhvaja and Khandikya Episode

When requested by Maitreya that he was desirous of being informed what was meant by the term yoga, Parashara narrated him the episode of Keshidhvaja and Khandikya. In the olden times there was a king named Dharmadhvaja Janaka who had two sons Amitadhvaja and Kritadhvaja. Kritadhvaja had a son named Keshidhvaja who was endowed with metaphysical knowledge. Amitadhvaja also had a son named Khandikya who was well-versed in the way of works. Both were always engaged in hostilities and ultimately Khandikya was expelled from his dominion by Keshidhvaja. Khandikya took refuse in the woods and mountains with a small group of followers. Keshidhvaja even though being knower of truth, performed yajnas to overcome death *(4/VI/6:7-12).*

While Keshidhvaja was engaged in his yajna performances, his cow of sacrifice was killed by a lion. So he inquired of the priests what form of penance would expiate the sin., The priest told him that they did not know and referred him to Kasheru. On inquiry Kasheru told him that he too did not know and referred him to Shunaka who in turn informed him that he was unable to answer the query and told him that only Khandikya his enemy could answer the query properly. Despite the severe enmity between them, Keshidhvaja decided to approach his brother. When Khandikya beheld him clad in deer-skin, he took his bow and said, "You have robbed me of my kingdom and are deserving death". To this Keshidhvaja told him that he was there to solve his doubts and had no hostile intention. The ministers of Khandikya advised him to kill Keshidhvaja but he thought by killing his brother no doubt he would be the king of earth but Keshidhvaja would enjoy the spiritual merit. Khandikya was not ready to sacrifice his spiritual merit and ultimately decided to tell his brother what he wished to know. Keshidhvaja told him about the death of his cow and demanded to know what penance he should perform. Khandikya explained to his brother the rite of expiation and then Keshidhvaja returned to his place with his brother's permission *(4/VI/6:13-35).*

Even on the completion of all yajnic duties, Keshidhvaja did not feel the sense of fulfilment and remained perturbed. Finally he realized that his perturbation was due to his non-payment of fees to his teacher - Khandikya. So he went to Khandikya. Khandikya upon Keshidhvaja's reappearance assumed his weapons to kill him but Keshidhvaja told him that he had gone there to offer his guru's gift. His ministers advised Khandikya to demand the whole kingdom back but he thought why a person should give up a spiritual merit for a temporary earthly kingdom. So he went back to his brother and said, "Is it true that you wish to make me a gift?" "Indeed I do", answered Keshidhvaja. Khandikya rejoined, "You are knower of the spiritual wisdom. Please communicate that wisdom to me. If you do so, you will have dicharged your debt to your preceptor". *(4/VI/6:36-50).*

Keshidhvaja asked Khandikya as to why he did not ask for the kingdom even though he was born in the warrior race. Khandikya replied, "It is the duty of the warrior to protect his subjects in peace, and to kill in fight the enemies of his sway. It is no fault that you should have taken my kingdom from one who was unable to defend it, to whom it was a bondage. To solicit gift is not the duty of a prince and warrior; and for these reasons I have not asked for your kingdom, nor made a demand which ignorance alone would have suggested. Those only who are destitute of knowledge, desire kingdoms, not such as I am". *(4/VI/7:2-7).*

Keshidhvaja congratulated him on this and explained to him the seed of ignorance and further advised that "There is but one cure of worldly sorrows, the practice of yoga; no other is known". Then Khandikya requested Keshidhvaja to explain to him the yoga. Keshidhvaja explained to him the yoga by the practice of which sages attain liberation. After hearing the discourse on the yoga, Khandikya said to Keshidhvaja that he had done all that was necessary for his real bliss. Having received suitable homage from Khandikya, Keshidhvaja returned to his city *(4/VI/7:101-102).*

For receiving knowledge Keshidhvaja, even though he was a mighty king, gave up false egoistic sense and approached his deadly enemy with all humility worthy of a student. He went to the abode of his future guru not as a king but as a disciple -- clad in deer skin and followed the time-honoured dictum 'Learn that (knowledge) through prostration, service and by asking questions'. Khandikya on the other hand subdued his anger and enmity and valued spiritual merits superior to earthly kingdom. The pupil was to show the very greatest respect to the teacher. It was not, however, merely a one-sided discipline. The teacher too observed certain vows and rules while he taught. The disciple was very much uneasy when he realized that he had not paid the fees to his Guru (which the Guru never expected). On his reappearance the Guru subdued his passion for the whole kingdom which he could have demanded and could have surely received and asked for the spiritual wisdom. Khandikya realized that it was no fault of Keshidhvaja who had taken his kingdom, as he was unable to defend it, 'to whom it was a bondage and who was thus freed from the encumbrance of ignorance'. Sense of possession that proceeds from human frailties, is not compatible with virtue. When thus the disciple became capable of discriminative knowledge, the Guru urged him 'to restrain his mind from all the objects of sense, and there-with meditate upon the supreme being'. The wisdom given by Keshidhvaja removed all impurity from Khandikya's mind. It is said, "Approach to the master destroys three demerits, viz. (1) crookedness, (2) jealousy, (3) lack of control by bowing down to, serving and asking questions to the master respectfully *(3:178)*. In this episode it blessed both the Guru and the disciple. Knowledge is virtue, intellectual congnitions of a person do and must mould his moral life.

COMMENCING DISCOURSE

The Purana is a discourse between the preceptor Parashara and the disciple Maitreya. Maitreya having revered his preceptor who had performed the morning rites of devotion said, "Master, I have been instructed by you in the whole of Vedas, and in the institutions of law and of sacred science through your favour, other men, even though they may be my foes cannot accuse me of having been remiss in the acquirement of knowledge" *(4/I/1:2-3)*. This implies that it was the sustained scholarship and close study that qualified Maitreya to receive the benevolent favour of his preceptor in the form of knowledge. Only by virtue of self- study and curiosity the pupil was qualified to receive knowledge from the teacher. When the learner is ready to acquire knowledge, then and then alone the teacher should impart knowledge. With humility the pupil would put his questions and doubts before the teacher and the teacher would give answers and clarify the doubts.

Maitreya requested his teacher to unfold before him the five topics contained in the ideal Purana. On this Parashara narrated to his disciple, his own experience. When Parashara heard that his father had been devoured by a Rakshasa employed by Vishvamitra, violent anger seized him and he commenced a sacrifice to demolish the Rakshasas. Hundreds of them were reduced to ashes by the rites. As they were on the verge of entire extirpation his grandsire Vasishtha spoke to him, "Enough my child, let your wrath be appeased, your father's death was the work of destiny. Anger is the passion of fools, it becomes not a wise man" *(4/I/1:16-17)*. Anger is the destruction of all that man obtains by arduous exertions,. of fame and devout austerities. Mercy is the might of the righteous. Thus advised by the grandsire, Parashara immediately desisted from the rite and the grandsire was content with him. Then arrived Pulastya, the son of Brahma who was received with reverence by his grandsire. Pulastya said to Parashara:

Since, in the violence of animosity, you have listened to the words of your progenitor, and have exercised clemency, therefore you shall become learned in every science; since you have forborne, even though incensed, to destroy my posterity, I will bestow upon you another boon, and you shall become the author of a summary of the Puranas *(4/I/1:24-26)*.

This specifically implies that it was the virtues which were imperative for receiving knowledge of any kind. The sages of the time were not inclined to impart knowledge to those who would turn the nectar of knowledge into heinous poison instrumental in the exploitation of the weak. Values are basic to education. They make man more humane.

The Spirit of a Nation

Each nation has a particular role to play in the world. The division of humanity into various nationalities each having a distinct character is the result of providential arrangement. Every nation is destined through its peculiar organization and its place in the world to represent a certain side of the divine image. Each nation has a special theme, a special national purpose.

According to the Vishnu Purana the country that lies north of the ocean, and south of the snowy mountains, is called Bharata, for there dwelt the descendents of Bharata. Bharata is the land of acts as a consequence of which men go to heaven, or obtain emancipation *(4/II/3:1)*. The Vishnu holds that Bharata is the best of the divisions of Jambu- dvipa and further states that even the gods themselves explained that, "Happy are those who are born as men in Bharatavarsha as that is the way to the final liberation" *(4/II/3:22, 24, 25)*. India's national purpose acording to the Vishnu is the development of spirituality to help each individual attain spiritual freedom.

Concept of Man

Human creation is termed as **Arvak-srotas** from the downward current (of their nutriment). They abound in the light of knowledge, but qualities of darkness and foulness (passion) predominate. Hence they are afflicted with evils, and are repeatedly impelled to action. They have knowledge both externally and internally, and are the instruments (of accomplishing the object of creation, the liberation of soul) *(4/I/5:17-18)*.

Indian tradition eulogizes man as the highest being on the earth. In the empiricial world man is the highest reality, as he approaches the Supreme Person closer than anything else. Because creation is purposeful and because man is potentially one with God, i.e. because realization is neither denied nor determined, the purpose of universe is moral -- man is free to realize or remain ignorant of his true nature, to follow or reject the law of his true being. Each man may choose to live by his true nature or disavow his true nature, and thereby also to disavow the moral purposefulness of life; but in either case, he alone is responsible. Thus the universe is moral and man is a responsible actor. So education is a necessity because without it man's intellectual and spiritual powers will not be awakened and guided in the direction of his growth and ultimate perfection.

End and Means

That which is the cause of a thing is called the means of effecting it; and that which is the desire of the soul to accomplish is the thing to be effected. For the yogi who is desirous of liberation, control over breath and the like are the means and the end is the supreme Brahman *(4/I/22:44- 45)*.

There are two states of the Brahman, one with, and one without shape, one perishable, and one imperishable; which are inherent in all beings. The imperishable is the supreme being; the perishable is the world. The blaze of fire burning on one spot diffuses light and heat around; so the world is nothing more than the manifested energy of the supreme Brahman *(4/I/22:55-56).*

The world at large is a reflection of a power of being above and beyond all the physical manifestation of nature. The child is a localization of this inner power, essentially in harmony with it, striving to develop under it, and curtailed only by the obstacles of ignorance and the constant intrusion of physical bodies that surround him. Education is the constant and systematic direction of the child as he unfolds the essentials of his spiritual nature. "Brahmanic India has traditionally insisted upon individual search and effort, upon free and unhampered development of the human soul to whatever spiritual goal it may lead" *(7:30- 31).*

Para and Apara Vidya

Knowledge is of two kinds, that which is derived from scriptures, and that which is derived from reflection. Spiritual knowledge consisting in words results from the study of science (Veda Shastra -- scripture) and the knowledge of the supreme results from reflection *(4/VI/5:61).* Brahman is of two kinds -- Shabda- Brahman, the Brahman to be attained through the word, that is, the Vedas and the duties they prescribe; and Para-Brahman, the Brahman to be attained through contemplation by which the difference betweern soul and matter is ascertained.

Ignorance is utter darkenss, to disperse it Vedic knowledge (Shruti) shines like lamp while contemplative wisdom shines like the sun *(4/VI/5:62).* The aspirant well-versed in the Vedic knowledge attains the Supreme Spirit. The Atharva Veda enjoins that there are two kinds of knowledge - Para and Apara (higher and lower); whatever knowledge such as arises from the Rig-veda etc. which ultimately helps the individual to attain the highest knowledge is termed as Apara Vidya and which leads the aspirant to the attainment of the Supreme is termed Para Vidya *(4/VI/5:64-65).* Hence the Brahman is the one end that is to be sought and realized.

It is for the welfare of the mankind that the divine has established the institution of Yajna which is the source of all happiness. Only the pure, dutiful, virtuous are capable of performing the Yajnas lawfully *(4/I/6:8-9)*.

To receive education in these two learnings one has to approach with sacrificial sticks Samidha in hand, the Master, abiding in Brahman and well-versed in the Vedas. The Master-introduces the child to scholarship and this is termed as Upanayana - the initiation of the child into scholarship. The student's life commences with the initiation.

Brahmacharya - the life of celibacy (studentship)

After the initiaiton the student has to prosecute his study of the Vedas diligently with an attentive spirit, and leading a life of continence. He has to wait upon his Guru, assiduously observant of purificatory practices. He has to study Vedas with steady mind and observing the religious vows. In the morning as well as in the evening he has to wait upon the Sun-God and the Fire-God with steady mind and pay his respects to his preceptor. He must stand when his master is standing; move when he is walking; and sit beneath him when he is seated; and must not do anything that is not agreeable to his preceptor. "When told by the master, let him read the Veda attentively sitting before the master, and let him eat the food he has collected as alms, when permitted by his master". He is to take bath after his teacher's bathing and must bring Samidha, water, Kusha-grass and flowers etc. for the teacher every morning. On the completion of his studies, the student is to enter into the order of householder with his teacher's consent and after having paid him the fees *(4/III/9:1-7)*.

The educational sysem of those days puts its insistence on truthfulness, observance of duty, devotion to the teacher and to one's parents, hospitality, faith and generosity. The numerous vows and observations obligatory on the Brahmacharin after the Upanayana, which was a kind of initiation by the teacher into a new spiritual life, entailed on him the most rigorous discipline for a prescribed period, during which he was to live religiously as a student in the house of his teacher. His daily routine is begging alms, collecting fuel, looking after the sacrificial fires, tending the house of the teacher, learning and practising austerities. The maintenance of chastity was obligatory on the Brahmacharin. Thus the ancient universities were residential and a perfect tutorial system was followed under the supervision of the teacher. The daily begging of alms, on which the student lived, had probably little to do with the financial status of the pupil or of the teacher with whom he resided.

Duties and Qualities of a Guru

The Brahmana should practise charity, worship Gods by performing Yajnas, should be assiduous in studies, should perform ablution and libations with water and should preserve sacred fire. For the subsistence he may perform Yajnas for others and instruct them in Shastras and he may accept wealth in accordance with social justice and morality. He must ever seek to promote the good of others, and do evil unto none, for the best riches of a Brahmana are universal benevolence. He should look upon the jewels of another person as if they were pebbles for him *(4/III/8:22-25)*.

The teachers were respected not for their material prosperity but for their wisdom, integrity and dedication to truth. They were free from avarice and wordly desires and endowed with noble qualities like goodness and tranquility. On assuming the role of a teacher persons would become curious of his qualities and duties and would subdue their passions for spiritual merit; all this is evident from the episode of Khandikya and Keshidhvaja. The teachers like Ribhu always thought of the ultimate welfare of their disciples and they saw to it that they did attain it.

Subjects of Study

The twenty-first chapter of the fifth book of the Vishnu refers to some of the subjects of study, viz. Dhanur-Veda with mystic part (mystic incantations); employment of weapons, four Vedas with their Angas. But as this was stated in reference to the student of warrior race, other subjects are not mentioned *(4/V/21:20-24)*.

Svadhyaya and Yoga

Svadhyaya (study of Vedas) and meditation were considered to be cause of attaining the Supreme. "From study let a man proceed to meditation, and from meditation to study; by perfection in both, supreme spirit becomes manifest". Study is one eye wherewith to behold it, and meditation is the other *(4/VI/6:1-3)*.

Upanishads emphatically enjoin that one should not be careless in his self-study and teaching.

Epistemology

"We offer salutation to that Supreme Hari who is one with the senses, both subtle and substantial, the recipient of all impressions, the root of all knowledge: to the universal soul, who, as internal organ, delivers the impressions received by the senses to soul" *(4/I/14:34-35)*.

These two stanzas have epistemological implications. Perception is a critical factor in human learning. The affections of external objects are carried by the outer instrument to their respective brain centres or organs, the organs carry the affections to the mind, the mind to the determinative faculty, from this the soul receives them, when perception results.

The actual mechanism of knowledge is very complex and elaborate. The mind is also called internal organ of knowledge (अंत:करण) hence it includes manas, buddhi, chitta, ahamkara, etc. *(10/I/---;121-22)*. The internal organ attends the objects, receives impressions and arranges them systematically. The internal organ undergoes modifications by assuminig different forms which reveal the objects of knowledge. The same internal organ discharges various functions and due to the differences of functions it is called mind, intellect, empirical ego (or self-sense) and attention. Radhakrishnan states that the internal organ is called manas when it has the mode of indetermination, buddhi when it has the mode of determination; ahamkara when it has the mode of self-conscious- ness; and chitta when it has the mode of concentration and remembrance *(8/II/---:486)*.

No animal is so supremely equipped to learn as is man. Central in this superb equipment is the human cerebrum. By virtue of it man can be matched by no other animal in flexibility and range of adaptation.

Self-Culture

It is the thesis of the Vishnu Purana that merits are basic to all prosperity-material, moral, spiritual. Accumulation of merits bestow all good. Worthiness results from amiableness, piety, good will and benevolence to all living creatures *(4/I/11:23-24)*. With avarice all beings become devoid of strength. Strength and prosperity go together. Without strength, where is excellence.[9] Without excellence there can be no vigour nor heroism, he who has neither courage nor energy will be spurned by all; and he who is universally treated with disgrace must suffer abasement of his intellectual faculties *(4/I/9:28-31)*.

(a) General Essential Moral-Merits

Tenderness towards all creatures, patience, humility, truth, purity, contentment, decency of decoration, gentleness of speech, friendliness, and freedom from envy and repining from avarice, and from detraction are the essential virtues common to all *(4/III/8:36-37)*.

(b) Sadachara

The term Sat means Sadhu (goodness) -- Sadhus are pious or just men -- and those practices which they follow are therefore Sadhacharas -- the observances of the pious *(4/III/11:3)*.

According to the Vishnu Purana the person who does not react sinfully to the sinful, speaks amicably to all men and whose heart melts with benevolance expels all sources of imperfection, and hence final felicity is in his grasp. The earth is upheld by the veracity of those who have subdued their passions, and, following righteous practices, are never contaminated by desire, covetousness, and wrath. So the Puran enjoins:

Let therefore a wise man ever speak the truth when it is agreeable and when the truth would inflict pain, let him hold his peace. Let him not utter that which, though acceptable, would be detrimental; for it were better to speak that which would be salutary, although it should give exceeding offence. A considerate man will always cultivate, in act, thought and speech that which is good for living beings, both in this world and in the next *(4/III/12:41- 45)*. Service to all living beings is the condition of man's full spiritual development. Moral heroism is the fruit of education.

REFERENCES

1. Jamanalal Bayti. *Reading in Education*. New Delhi: Uppal Publishing House, 1986.
2. John S. Brubacher. *Modern Philosophies of Edcuation* (fourth edition). Bombay: Tata McGraw-Hill, 1969.
3. P.B. Gajendragadkar (ed.). *The Ten Classicial Upanishads*, Vol. I. Bombay: Bharatiya Vidya Bhavan, 1981.
4. Munilal Gupta (ed. and translator). *Shri Shri Vishnu Purana* (Original Text with Hindi Translation) (3rd edition). Gorakhpur: Geeta Press, 1933.
5. R.C. Majumdar (ed.). *The Vedic Age*. London: Geroge Allen and Unwin Ltd., 1951.
6. R.C. Majumdar (ed.). *The Age of Imperial Unity*. Bombay: Bharatiya Vidya Bhavan, 1951.
7. Mehdi Nakosteen. *A Three-Fold Philosophy of Education*. Denver: Colo: Charles Mapes Publishing Co., 1943.
8. S. Radhakrishnan. *Indian Philosophy*, Vol. II, New York: McMillan, 1951.
9. S.M. Rakhe. *Educational Philosophy of Lokamanya Tilak and Swami Vivekananda - A Comparative Study*. Rajkot: Unpublished Doctoral Dissertation, 1981.
10. B.G. Tilak. *Complete Work*, Vols. I and III. Pune: Kesari Prakashan, 1976.
11. H.H. Wilson. *The Vishnu Purana -- A System of Hindu Mythology and Tradition*. Calcutta: Punthi Pustak, 1972.

ABBREVIATIONS

AA.	Aitareya Aranyaka
AB.	Aitareya Brahmana
AGS.	Ashvalayana Grihya Sutra
APDS.	Apastamba Dharma Sutra
APGS.	Apastamba Grihya Sutra
ArB.	Arsheya Brahmana
AV.	Atharva-Veda
BauDS.	Baudhayana Dharma Sutra
BOGS.	Bodhayana Grihya Sutra
BU.	Brihdaranya Upanishad
ChU.	Chandogya Upanishad
GDS.	Gautama Dharma Sutra
GGS.	Gobhila Grihya Sutra
KauGS.	Kaushitaka Grihya Sutra
KauU.	Kaushitaki Upanishad
KS.	Kathaka Samhita
MGS.	Manava Grihya Sutra
MS.	Manu Smriti
PGS.	Paraskara Grihya Sutra
RV.	Rigveda
ShB.	Shatapatha Brahmana
ShGS.	Shankhyayana Grihya Sutra
TA.	Taittiriya Aranyaka
TB.	Taittiriya Brahmana
TS.	Taittiriya Samhita
TU.	Taittiriya Upanishad
VB.	Vajaseniya Brahmana
VS.	Vajaseniya Samhita
VSS.	Vaikhanasa Smarta Sutra

INTRODUCTION

The frog hymn of the RV. (VII-103) gives a graphic picture of instructional system of education of Rigvedic age. The fifth verse runs as 'When one of these frogs follows another in making a noise just as a learner repeats the words of the teacher'. The verse gives a glimpse of the earliest Vedic school by the comparison of the croaking of the frogs to the chorous of voices heard when a teacher recites the Veda, section by section, and the pupils repeat his words after him. The first verse of the hymn suggests that this concerned school-recitation sprang into life suddenly, at a stated time as frogs raising their (rain-inspired) voices at the opening of the monsoon after lying low for (the rest of) the year are compared to Brahmanas conforming to their fixed annual routine (Vrata) (13:391). The entire instruction is given orally.

In the age of the later Samhitas, Vedic literature had grown into vast proportion and so the problem of the preservation of this literature became very acute as during this age the whole Vedic literature -- Samhitas, Brahmanas, Aranyakas, Upanishads -- was revered as Shruti or revealed literature. As the Vedic literature formed the main bulk of study, the process of imparting the knowledge of the sacred hymnology and sacrificial ritual must have been systematized during this age.

The ShB. (XI-5,6,8), TA. (II-9) and ChU. (VII-1-2,4,7.1) contain comprehensive lists of subjects of study. Obviously more emphasis was laid on the preservation of this literature by means of recitation. Memory was considered to be a valued faculty which was to be diligently cultivated. The ShB, emphatically enjoins that one should perform Svadhyaya regularly without interruption स्वाध्यायोऽ ध्येतव्यः। The Svadhyaya was considered as sacrifice to the Brahman.

The TS. (VI-3-10) refers to studentship, by which the debt to Rishis or to culture had to be paid. So one who continues his self-study (Svadhyaya) was called "the Rishis' treasure-warden"

(6/I/191). The end of formal studentship is not the end of education. In the TU, the teacher exhorts his parting pupil, 'not to neglect study, learning and teaching of the Veda' (I-2). It was imperative for the twice-born to study and teach without any desire of reward.[1]

It is the Svadhyaya that enables persons to understand and perform sacrifices, penance and auspicious acts and hence it is the highest bliss. Such an eulogy of Svadhyaya could positively motivate persons to undertake a study of its concept as described in the Vedic and post-Vedic literature.

The present study of Svadhyaya was undertaken with the following objectives:

(1) To study the importance of Svadhyaya as described in the Vedic and post-Vedic literature.

(2) To study the importance of Svadhyaya in all four orders.

(3) To study the method of Svadhyaya.

(4) To study the method of the teaching of the Veda.

---

11. ब्राह्मणेन निष्कारणो धर्मः षड़ङ्गो वेदोध्येयो ज्ञेय इति। पा. महाभाष्य।

(Vol. I, p. 1).

METHOD

The main sources of the data were (I) the original texts of Samhitas of the Yajurveda -- (1) Taittiriya, (2) Vajaseniya - Madhyandini and Kanva, (3) Kathaka, (4) Maitrayani; (II) the original texts of Brahmanas -- (1) Aitereya, (2) Tandya, (3) Shatapatha, (4) Shankhyayana, (5) Taittiriya; (III) the original texts of Aranyakas -- (1) Aitereya, (2) Taittiriya, (3) Shankhyayana; (IV) the original texts of Upanishads -- (1) Chhandogya, (2) Taittiriya; (V) the original texts of Dharma-Sutras -- (1) Apastamba, (2) Gautama; (VI) the original texts of Grihya-Sutras -- (1) Ashvalayana, (2) Shankhyayana, (3) Bodhayana, (4) Kaushitaka; (VII) (1) Vaikhanasa Smarta Sutra; (VIII) the original text of the Smritis -- (1) Manu, (2) Vishnu, (3) Yajnavalkya; (IX) the original text of the Rigvedic Pratishakhya.

The following commentaries and translations of the Samhitas, Brahmanas, Aranyakas, Upanishads, Dharma-Sutras, Grihya-Sutras and Smritis were of immense help to the author for the English rendering of the portions of these works which were referred to in this study as well as for their analysis:

Commentaries

Taittiriya Samhita	- Sayanacharya
Tandya Maha Brahmana	- Sayanacharya
Taittiriya Brahmana	- Sayanacharya
Aitereya Aranyaka	- Sayanacharya
Taittiriya Aranyaka	- (i) Sayanacharya, and (ii) Bhattabhaskara
Chhandogya Upanishad	- (i) Anandgiri, and (ii) Shankara

Translations (English, Hindi and Marathi)

Taittiriya Samhita	- A.B. Keith
Shatapatha Brahmana	- Julius Eggeling
Shatapatha Brahmana (Hindi)	- G.P. Upadhyaya
Chhandogya Upanishad (Marathi)	- C.G. Bhanu

Thirteen Upanishads - F. Max Muller
Taittiriya Upanishad - Alladi Mahadeo Shastri
Apastamba Dharma Sutra - Geroge Buhler
The Grihya Sutras (13) - Herman Oldenberg

The material has been discussed under the following heads:

(i) Importance of knowledge
(ii) Importance of Svadhyaya (Vedic literature)
(iii) The term 'Svadhyaya'
(iv) Svadhyaya in the Brihaddevata
(v) Svadhyaya in the Dharma Sutras
(vi) Svadhyaya in the Grihya Sutras
(vii) Svadhyaya in the Smritis
(viii) The method of Svadhyaya
(ix) The four Veda-Vratas
(x) The method of teaching the Veda
(xi) The Upakarma, Utsarga and Anadhyaya

IMPORTANCE OF KNOWLEDGE

Numerous Vedic passages state that the aim of the priest is to obtain preeminence in ब्रह्मवर्चसम् [1] (10/I/:86) – spiritual preeminence resulting from sacred knowledge. आ ब्रह्मन् ब्राह्मणो ब्रह्मवर्चसी जायताम् । (TS. VII-5, 18, 1)

'In the priesthood may a Brahmana be born of spiritual glory' (9/II/:633).

Sayana comments, ब्रह्मन् ब्राह्मणजातौ ब्रह्मवर्चसी श्रुताध्ययनसंपन्नो आजायताम् । (TS./VIII/:4745)

आ ब्रह्मन् ब्राह्मणो ब्रह्मवर्चसी जायतामित्याह । ब्राह्मण एव ब्रह्मवर्चसं दधाति । तस्मात् पुरा ब्राह्मणो ब्रह्मवर्चस्यजायत, इति । (TB. III-8, 13, 1)

In the ShB. there is a passage, "Who is that walketh singly? -- It is yonder sun, doubtless, that walketh singly, and he is ब्रह्मवर्चसम्: ब्रह्मवर्चसाग् the two (priests) thus bestow on him" (XIII-2, 6, 10; 5/V/:314-15).

---

1 — A.B. Keith takes it as, 'Spiritual glory' (9/II/:633).
— Sayana as, 'Well-versed in the Vedic lore' (TS. : 1198).
—Julius Eggeling as, '(i) spiritual lustre, (ii) holy lustre, (iii) inspired nature' (5/V/:314-15).
— V.S. Apte as, (i) divine glory or splendour, (ii) spiritual preeminence or holiness resulting from sacred-knowledge, (iii) the inherent sanctity or power of a Brahmana (6:706).
—Monier Williams as, '(i) a divine glory or splendour, (ii) preeminence in holiness or sacred knowledge, (iii) sanctity, (iv) superhuman power' (15:739)

Many rituals are specified as leading to Brahmavarchasam -- according to the KS. (37-7) - Sacrifice with the Brihaspati--Sava leads to Brahmavarchasam.[1] The TB. (2-7-1) recommends - Trivritstoma among the prayer that surely leads to Brahmavarchasam.[2] There is also a passage in the SB. (II-3, 1, 31):

तदुहैतदेवाऽरुणये। ब्रह्मवर्चसकामाय तक्षाऽन् वा चाऽग्निर्वर्चोज्योतिर्वर्चः सूर्यो वर्चो ज्योतिर्वर्च इति। ब्रह्मवर्चसीहैव भवति य एवं विद्वानग्निहोत्रं जुहोति।

"Here now Takshan recited for Aruni who wished to obtain holy lusture (Brahmavarchasam)[3], 'Agni is lustre, light is lustre' -- Surya is lustre. Holy lustre, therefore, he obtains whoever, knowing this, thus offers the Agnihotra" (5/I/:335).

But the solemn ritual that leads to Brahmavarchasam is the study of the scriptures continued day by day without interruption - स्वाध्याय। Probably the earliest mention of Svadhyaya is found in the ShB.:

यः समिद्धारो वा स्वाध्यायं वा विसृजते। (III 4,3,6) अथेतरे विसृज्यन्ते समिद्धारा वा स्वाध्यायं वा न भागा।

(IV-6, 9, 7).

> "Now, while the gods were consecrated, whichever of them fetched fire-wood or uttered his appointed texts (5/II/:98).

---

1. स एष बृहस्पतिसवो ब्रह्मवर्चसकाम एतेन यजेत ब्रह्मवर्चसी भवति तस्यैषैव नियतिः प्रजास्सर्वा ब्राह्मणीर्ब्रह्मवर्चसिनीर्भवन्ति।

2. त्रिवृत्स्तोमो भवति।ब्रह्मवर्चसं वै त्रिवृत्। ब्रह्मवर्चसमेवावरून्धे।।

Sayana comments : सर्वेषु स्तोत्रेषु त्रिवृत्स्तोभ एकः कर्तव्यः। तस्य ब्रह्मवर्चस-हेतुत्वाद् ब्रह्मवर्चस प्राप्तिर्भवति।

(TB. : 694).

3. अग्निर्ज्योतिर्ज्योतिरग्निः स्वाहा सूर्यो ज्योतिर्ज्योतिः सूर्यः स्वाहा। अग्निर्वर्चो ज्योतिर्वर्चः स्वाहा सूर्यो वर्चो ज्योतिर्वर्चः स्वाहा। ज्योतिः सूर्यः सूर्यो ज्योतिः स्वाहा।

(VS. 3-9)

"Then the others are dismissed, either for fetching fuel or to their day's reading of the scripture" (5/II/:448).

The ShB. also states that one is bound to study (the Veda), for that reason he is born as (owing) a debt to the Rishis : hence it is to them that he does this for one who has studied (the Veda) they call "the Rishi's treasure-warden" (5/I/191).

The TA. (II:10-13) has dealt with Svadhyaya or Brahmayajna at length. TA.II-10 is identical to the ShB. passages on Svadhyaya (XI-5, 6, 3-8) except that in the TA. the Atharvangiras are said to be honey offerings and Brahmana texts, Itihasa, Puranas, Kalpas (works on Shrauta ritual) and Gatha Narasamsi are said to be fat offering, and the rewards bestowed by the gods are long life, brilliance, lustre, prosperity.[1]

The TU. puts Svadhyaya on the level of 'tapas' and exhorts the student on the eve of his return home not to neglect his Svadhyaya (I-9). In the ChU. there is a reference to Svadhyaya:
अथातः शौव उद्गीथस्तद्ध बको दाल्भ्यो ग्लावो वा मैत्रेयः स्वाध्यायमुद्वव्राज ।

(I-12, 1).

'He went out of the village to perform his Svadhyaya'. The Kau U. episode runs as: Chitra Gargayani chose Aruni to be his priest to perform a sacrifice for him. But Aruni sent his son Shvetaketu. When Shvetaketu arrived, Chitra asked him a very obscure question, the answer of whch Shvetaketu did not know. So he approached his sire and on inquiry Aruni said:
अहमप्येतन्नवेद सदस्येव वयं स्वाध्यायमधीत्य हरामहे यन्नः परे ददत्येहयुभौ गमिष्याव इति ।

(I-2)

"I also do not know this. Only after having learnt the proper portion of the Veda in Chitra's own dwelling, shall we obtain what others give us (knowledge). Come, we will both go" (14/I/:273).

---

1. अथर्वाङ्गिरसो मध्वाहुतिभिर्यद् ब्राह्मणानीतिहासान्पुराणानि कल्पान्गाथा नाराशंसीर्मेदाहुतिभिरेव तद् देवाँस्तर्पयति त एनं तृप्ता आयुषा वर्चसा श्रिया यशसा ब्रह्मवर्चसेन्नाद्येन च तर्पयन्ति ।

(II-10).

IMPORTANCE OF SVADHYAYA

The ShB. enumerates स्वाध्याय as ब्रह्मयज्ञ among the list of five great sacrifices or sacrificial sessions. So the daily study of the scriptural lesson is a sacrifice continued day by day. The student is a sacrificer during the sacrifice (during period of his Vedic study or for life). The Brahmana further states that the juhu-spoon of this Brahmayajna is speech, its Upabhrit the mind, its Dhruva the eye, its Sruva mental power, its purificatory bath truth, its conclusion heaven[1] (5/V/:95-96).

The Rik-texts are milk-offerings to the gods, so the student who studies them for his lesson satisfies the gods with milk-offerings; and being satisfied, the gods satisfy him by granting him security of possession, by life-breath, by seed, by his whole self, and by all auspicious blessings. One who studies the Yajus-texts for his lesson satisfies the gods with ghee-offerings; with the study of the Saman-texts for his lesson he satisfies the gods with Soma-offerings; with the study of Atharvangiras he satisfies the gods with fat-offerings and with his study of the precepts, the sciences, the dialogue, the traditional myths and legends and the Narasamsi Gathas, he satisfies the gods with honey- offerings. For each of these studies the gods satisfy the student by all auspicious blessing (XI-5, 4-8). The ShB, while explaining the importance of Svadhyaya says that the study and teaching are a source of pleasure to him (who performs Svadhyaya everyday), he becomes ready-minded, and independent of others, and day by day he acquires wealth. He sleeps peacefully; he is the best physician for himself; and (peculiar) to him are restraint of the senses, delight in the one thing, growth of intelligence, fame, and the (task of) perfecting the people. Not

---

1. अथ ब्रह्मयज्ञः। स्वाध्यायो वै ब्रह्मयज्ञस्तस्य वा एतस्य ब्रह्मयज्ञस्य वागेव जुहूर्मन उपभृधक्षुर्ध्रुवा मेधा स्रुवः सत्यमवमृथः स्वर्गो लोक उदयनम्।

(XI-5,6:3).

only that whatever may be the toils here between heaven and earth, the study (of the scriptures) is their last stage, their goal (limit) for him who, knowing this, studies his lesson, and verily whatever portion of the sacred poetry he studies, for his lesson with that sacrificial rite, offering is made by him whosoever studies his lesson regularly. If he studies his lesson, even though lying on a soft couch, anointed, adorned and completely satisfied, he is burned (with holy fire) upto the tips of his nails whosoever studies his lesson daily. The Brahmana further declares that the Rik-texts, truly, are honey, the Saman-texts ghee, and the Yajus-texts ambrosia; and, indeed, when he studies the dialogue that (speech and reply) is a mess of milk and a mess of meat and with the study of each of them he satisfies the gods with the different offerings as mentioned and in turn the gods satisfy him by every object of desire, by every kind of enjoyment (5/V/:99-101; XI-5, 7, 1-9). So the Brahmana enjoins that:

> Moving, indeed, are the waters, moving is the sun, moving the moon, and moving the stars, and, verily, as if these deities did not move and act, even so will the Brahmana be on that day on which he does not study his lesson; therefore one's (daily) lesson should be studied. And hence let him at least pronounce either a Rik-verse or a Yajus-formula, or a Saman-verse, or a Gatha, or a Kumbhya[1] to ensure continuity of the Vrata (5/V/:101; XI-5, 7, 10).

So whosoever performs his Svadhyaya day by day gains an imperishable world which is thrice or more of the world he gains by giving away (to the priest) the earth replete with wealth (5/V/96).

According to the TA.[2] untouched by evil is Svadhyaya. It is, verily, the purifier even of the Devas. He that castes it aside, is

---

1. A Kumbhya according to Sayana is a Brahmana-passage explanatory of some sacrificial rite but in his commentary on AU. II, 3,6,8 he takes it as a verse conveying some precept of conduct (5/V/:101 note).
2. यस्तित्याज सखिविदं सखायं न तस्य वाच्यपि भागो अस्ति। यदीं शृणोत्यल्कं शृणोति न हि प्रवेद सुक्रतस्य पन्थामिति। (11-15)

not lucky (even) in speech; no share has he in heaven (II-15). The TA. further states that [1] whosoever performs his Svadhyaya even when it rains and lightens, when the wind is blowing, even on the new moon day, he only practises penance because 'study, indeed, is penance' (II- 14). Not only that "Standing or walking, sitting or lying down, he shall not fail to recite the Veda; then he is a man of penance, he is pure, who, thus knowing, recites the Veda[2]" (II-12). Wherefore, as productive of great fruits,[3] it is a penance higher even than the penance of fasting and giving away wealth. So the TA, declares[4]:

> What measure of Svarga he wins who gives away this earth full of wealth, that measure of the world he (who studies the Veda) wins, (a world) which is even greater and inexhaustible. He, moreover, conquers death, he attains unity with Brahman (II-14).

The TA further enjoins that if a man is unable to go out of village he may perform Svadhyaya by revolving in his mind in the village itself the Veda by day or even by night. Thus spake

1. य एवं विद्वान् मेघे वर्षति विद्योतमाने स्तनयत्यवस्फूर्जति पवमाने वायावमावास्यायां स्वाध्यायमधीते तप एव तत्तप्यते तपो हि स्वाध्याय इति। (II-14).

2. उतारण्येऽबल उत वाचो त तिष्ठन्नुत व्रजन्नुतासीन उत शयानो ऽधीयीतैव स्वाध्यायं तपस्वी पुण्यो भवति य एवं विद्वान् स्वाध्यायमधीते। (II-12).

3. Cf. ShB. (XI-5, 7, 9) "Now, for this sacrifice to the Brahman there are four Vashat calls (with which at the end of the offering-formula, the oblation is poured into the fire) to wit, when it thunders, and when it rumbles; whence he who knows this should certainly study when the wind is blowing, and when it lightens, or thunders, or rumbles, so as not to lose his Vashat-calls; and verily he is freed from recurring death, and attains to community of nature (or being) with the Brahman. And should he be altogether unable (to study), let him at least read a single divine word; and thus he is not shut out from beings (5/V/:99).

4. उत्तमं नाकं रोहत्युत्तमस्समानानां भवति यावन्तं ह वा इमां वित्तस्य पूर्णां ददत्स्वर्गं लोकं जयति भूयांसं चाक्षय्यं चाप पुनर्मृत्युं जयति ब्रह्मणस्सायुज्यं गच्छति। (II-14).

the seer Shauch the son of Shuchi (II-12). The principal matter is one should study the lesson day by day without any interruption -- time and place being quite subordinate.

Shankara in his commentary on the TU. (IX-1) explains Svadhyaya as learning of one's own Veda and Pravachana as a daily solemn recitation of it. Svadhyaya is the necessary study intended for retention of the text in memory as well as for increase of merit.

The terms 'Upasana' (उपासना) and Svadhyaya have similar connotation. While discussing the term Upasana, Sayana in his commentary on the TU. states that just as, in pursuance of the scriptural command that everyone should learn his own scriptures, one recites the Vedic text frequently till he can fix it in memory, so, the thought should be often repeated. If the very word 'adhyayana' means repeated utterances, the word 'upasana' also means a frequent repetition of thought (TA:56). So Svadhyaya is a contemplative study carried on day by day; and continued intently, never swerving from it.

Sayana while commenting on the (IX-1) of the TU. says that even the sannyasin who renounces all former works, even he should not abandon Svadhyaya. But the Aruni U.[1] categorically enjoins the abandonment even of Svadhyaya (and also the Paramahansa U.)[2]. According to Sayana this objection does not apply here. For the Shruti enjoins that the ritualistic section of the Veda, which is of no use to the sannyasin, should be alone abandoned. A repeated study, however, of the useful portion is necessary, as the same U. (Aruni) mentions it[3] as one of the sannyasin's duties, in the following words:

> He shall first take a bath at the three connecting periods, he shall hold communion with Atman in samadhi; he shall often repeat the Aranyakas of all the Vedas; he shall repeat the Upanishad, aye shall he repeat the Upanishad (I-2).

---

1. शिखां यज्ञोपवीतं च यागं च सूत्रं च स्वाध्यायं च ——— विसर्जयेत्। (I-1).

2. स्वाध्यायं च सर्वकर्माणि ——— हित्वा। (I-1).

3. त्रि संध्यादौ स्नानमाचरेत् संधिं समाधावात्मन्याचरेत् सर्वेषु वेदेष्वारण्यकमावर्त येदुपनिषदमावर्तयेदुपनिषदमावर्तयेत्। (1-2)

So none should give up Svadhyaya and Pravachana -- that is special regard should be paid to these duties -- this is indicated by the repetition (13 times) in the TU. (IX-1) of the words 'study and teaching'.

स्वाध्याय प्रवचने एवेति नाको मौद्गल्यः । तद्धि तपस्तद्धि तपः । (TU. IX-2).

"Study and teaching alone, as Naka, the son of Mudgala, holds; that, verily is penance, aye that is penance".

The seer named Naka, the son of Mudgala thinks that study and teaching should alone be practised, as they constitute themselves a penance. So they alone should be practised. Sayana explains that Naka is so called because, always contended with the study and recitation of the Vedas, he never felt any sort of anguish. Yajniki U. delcares that penance is the most important as by penance Devas were first to go to God; by penance did Rishis attain Svarga (79). But this does not, however, detract from the validity of Maudgalya's contention that study and the recitation of the Vedas are the most important. They alone constitute the highest penance and therefore they are termed as Brahmayajna and should be practised even on those days on which the first learners should not study the Veda CTA.III/:530).

THE TERM 'SVADHYAYA'

स य एवं विद्वान् अनुशासनानि विद्यां वाकोवाक्यमितिहासपुराणं गाथा नारशंसीरित्यरहरहः स्वाध्यायमधीते मध्वाहुतिभिरेव तद् देवांस्तर्पयति ।

(ShB.XI-5, 6, 8).

> "Whosoever studies day by day the precepts[1], the sciences[2], the dialogue[3] (theological discussions) the traditional myths and legends[4], and the Narasamsi Gathas[5] (stanzas in praise of heroes), for his lesson, satisfies the gods with honey-offerings".

If the different subjects stated in the above-mentioned passage of the ShB. and also in the TA. (II-9) for the perusal in Svadhyaya are taken into consideration, the meaning of the term Svadhyaya is to be taken in its comprehensive reference. Svadhyaya is a contemplative study carried on day by day, continued intently, never swerving from it.

The Vedic Index defines Svadhyaya as, "(reciting to oneself) in Brahmanas denotes the study or repetition of the Vedic texts" (11/II:496). According to Apte's dictionary it means, "Self-recitation; (1) muttering to oneself; (2) study of the Vedas, sacred

---

1. Sayana takes them as Vedangas or rules of grammar.

2. Philosophical systems.

3. Some special theological discourse like Brahmodya.

4. Cosmological myths (Itihasa), story of Pururavas and Urvashi (Purana).

5. 'Verses telling about men' (5/V/:98). Bhattabhaskara Mishra takes इतिहास as महाभारतादयः । पुराणानि ब्रह्माण्डानि । यद्व-इतिहास परकृतयः 'देवासुरास्संयत्ता आसन्' इत्यादयः । पुराणानि पुराकल्पाः । इदं वा अग्रे' इत्यादयः । गाथाः गायति चोदिता मन्त्रविशेषाः 'यमगाथाभिः परिगायति' इत्यादिभिः । ---- नराशंसस्ये मा नाराशंस्यः होता यक्षन्नराशंसं इत्याद्याः ।

(II-9, 229).

study, perusal of sacred books; (3) the Veda itself; (4) a day on which sacred study is enjoined to be resumed after suspension" (6/III/:17,36). Raja Radhakantdev in his शब्द कल्पद्रुम refers to Svadhyaya as, " सुष्ठु आवृत्य अध्यायः वेदाध्ययनम्। आवृत्य वेदाध्ययनम्"। तत्पर्यायः। जपः। इत्यमरः। 2/7/47 (18/V/:491). According to Monier Williams it is, "reciting or repeating or rehearsing to onself, repetition or recitation of the Veda in a low voice to oneself; repeating the Veda aloud, recitation or perusal of any sacred texts" (15:1277).

SVADHYAYA IN THE BRIHADDEVATA

There are three verses in the Brihaddevata where there is a reference to Svadhyaya - VI-133; 143, VIII-133.

उत्तरे च य इत्येते स्वाध्यायाध्येतृसंस्तवः । (VI-133)

"The two next (that is RV. IX-67, 31, 32) are (in) praise of the student of recitation".

cp. Sarvanukramani to pavamany-adhyetru-stuti (RV.IX-67-31, 32 begin with the words yah pavamanir adhyeti) (12/II/:244).

The stanzas 31 and 32 run as:

(31) The man who reads the essence stored by saints (Rishis), the Pavamani hymns, tastes food completely purified, made sweet by Matarishvan's touch.

(32) Whosoever reads the essence stored by saints, the Pavamani hymns, Sarasvati draws forth for him water and butter, milk and meat.

(7:497)

अनुसूयुरधीयानः शुश्रुषुस्तपसान्वितः । दशपूर्वापरान् वश्यान् पुनात्यात्मानमेव च । (VI-142)

पापं यच्चाकरोत्किंचित् मनोवाग्देहभोजनैः । पूतः स तस्मात् सर्वस्मात्
स्वाध्यायफलमन्श्रुते । (VI-143)

"One who is not envious, is studious, obedient, and practises penance, purifies ten ascendents and descendants as well as himself".

"And whatever sin he has committed with mind, speech, body, and food - purified from all that, he enjoys *the fruit of Vedic study*". Rigvidhana (III-2-5) says: Svādhyāya punyam atulam putah prāpnoti cakṣayam (12/II/:247).

स्वाध्यायमपि योऽधीते मन्त्रदैवत विच्छुचिः ।
स सत्रसदिव स्वर्गे सत्रसद्भिरपीड़यते । (VIII-133).

"He who knowing the divinities of the formulas, being pure, also devotes himself to study, is, like one seated at a sacrificial session in heaven, lauded even by those who are engaged in such a session" (12/II:132).

It is clear from the above verses that the merits of Svadhyaya are unmatched by any merit that acrues to a person by other religious rites. Its merit is considered to be the highest. While illustrating the merits which a person gets by the study of the Brahmana and by knowing the names and family names of the Rishis the Arsheya Brahmana says that the person who comprehends the names and the family names of the Rishis will be the guest of each of the Rishis for one thousand years of the gods and having been thus honoured, will enjoy the merits of Svadhyaya (I/i, 5).

It is asserted that the joy of the Shrotriya (श्रोत्रिय)[1] -- an accomplished student of the Veda -- is equal to the highest joy possible. "What is a hundred times the bliss of Prajapati, that is one bliss of Brahman, as also of a Shrotriya, not smitten by desire" (TU.VIII-13). This is the highest bliss.

A student of all three Vedas being called tri-Shukriya (त्रिशुक्रिय) or tri-Shukra (त्रिशुक्र) thrice pure (11/II/:86).

त्रयी वै विद्या । ऋचो यजूंषि सामानि ----------
सैषा त्रयी विद्या सोम्येऽध्वरे प्रयुज्यते । (ShB. IV-6, 7, 1).

सैषा त्रयी एव विद्या तपति । (ShB.X-5, 2, 2).

त्रिवृत्स्तोमो ब्रह्मवर्चसं वै त्रिवृद् ब्रह्मवर्चसेनैवाभिषिच्यते । (KS.XXXVI-7).

त्रिवृत्स्तोमो भवति । ब्रह्मवर्चसं वै त्रिवृत्[।ब्रह्मवर्चसमेवावरून्धे । ।१ । ।
अरुणोमिर्भिरस्मि शुक्रः एतद्वै ब्रह्मवर्चसस्य रूपम् । रूपेणैव ब्रह्मवर्चसमवरून्धे । ।२ । ।

(TB.II-7, 1-2).

---

1. ते ये शतं प्रजापतेरानन्दाः । स एको ब्रह्मण आनन्दः । श्रोत्रियस्य चाकामहतस्य ।

(TU. VIII-1, also BU.IV-3,33).

A special form of disputation was the Brahmodya, for which there was a regular place at the horse sacrifice and at the ten-day festival[1] (11/I/87). The reward of learning was gaining the title of Kavi or Vipra or sage[2] (11/I/87). The ShB. states:[3]

> The priests of the priest, of the great inspirer of devotion -- the learned Brahmanas versed in sacred writ, truly, are the priests : it is regarding them that he says this. And 'of the great inspirer of devotion' -- the great inspirer of devotion, truly, is the sacrifice : it is regarding the sacrifice that he says this. 'The knower of rites alone hath assigned the priestly offices', for, in performing the sacrifice, they indeed assign the priestly offices. 'Great the praise of the divine Savitri, Hail'! Thus he offers to Savitri for his impulsion (5/II/:129-30).

---

1. अथ वाको वाक्ये ब्रह्मोद्यं वदन्ति। सर्वं वै तेषामाप्तं भवति।

(ShB.IV-6,9,20; also XIII-5, 2, 11).

2. अग्ने महाँ असि ब्राह्मण भारत। असावसौ। देवेद्धोमन्विद्ध।
ऋषिष्टुतो विप्रानुमदितः। कविशस्तो ब्रह्मसँशितो धृताहवनः।।

(TB.III-5, 3, 1; also TS.II-5, 9, 1).

3. विप्रः विप्रस्य बृहतो विपश्चितः इति। ये वै ब्राह्मणाः शुश्रुवाँ सोऽनू चानास्ते विप्रास्तानेवै तदभ्याह बृहतो विपश्चित इति यज्ञो वै बृहन्विपश्चिद्यज्ञमेवैतदभ्याह विहोत्रा दधे वयुनाविदेकऽ इदिति विहि होत्रा दधते यज्ञं तन्वाना मही देवस्य सवितुः परिष्टुतिः स्वाहेति तत्सावित्रं प्रसवाय जुहोति।

(ShB. III-5, 3, 12).

SVADHYAYA IN THE DHARMA SUTRAS

Among the Dharma Sutras which are consulted in this study, it is the APDS that discusses Svadhyaya in detail. In (I- 2,5) it states that the word *tapas* must be understood to apply to the observances of the rules of studentship. The student should not transgress these rules and study otherwise he loses his capacity for learning. He will go to hell and his life will be shortened; not only that on account of that no Rishis are born amongst the men of later age. But some in their new birth, on account of a residue of the merit acquired by their actions (in former lives), become (similar to) Rishis by their knowledge (of the Veda), like Shvetaketu (1-6). The duties of a student consist in acts to please the spiritual teacher, the observance (of rules) conducive to his own welfare, and industry in studying. Act other than these need not be performed by a student. If the student retains what he has learnt, finds pleasure in the fulfilment of the law, keeps the rules of studentship and remains upright and forgiving, he surely attains perfection (9-11). He shall be very attentive the whole day long, never allowing his mind to wander from the lesson during the (time devoted to) studying (24). And during the time for rest (he shall give) his mind (to doubtful passages of the lesson learnt) (26)[1] (2/I/:18-22).

---

1. नियमेषु तपः शब्दः ।।१।। तदतिक्रमे निःस्त्रवति ब्रह्मसहापत्यादेतस्मात् ।।२।। कर्तपत्यमनायुष्यं च ।।३।। तस्माद् ऋषयोवरेषु न जायन्ते नियमातिक्रमात् ।।४।। श्रुतर्षयस्तु भवन्ति केचित् कर्मफलशेषेण पुनः संभवे ।।५।। यथा श्वेतकेतुः !।६।। गुरू प्रसादनीयानि कर्माणि स्वस्तयनमध्ययनसंवृत्ति।रिति ।।७।। अतोन्यानि निवर्तन्ते ब्रह्मचारिणः कर्माणि ।।२०।। स्वाध्यायधृग्धर्मरूचिस्तपस्व्यृजुर्मृदुः सिध्यति ब्रह्मचारी ।।११।। सर्वाहणं सुयुक्तोध्ययन्तरोध्याये ।।२३ (२४)।। मनसा चानध्याये ।।२५ (२६)।।

1. cf. TA.II-11, 10, 1 scq.; also ShB.XI-5, 6, 1.

The APDS further enjoins that Svadhyaya is tapas and quotes the TA. (II-12, 3 and 15, 3(2)). In the third Sutra it quotes the ShB. (XI-5, 6, 8(3)). In the fifth it states that:

> Now, if the wind blows, or if it thunders, or if lightening flashes, or thunderbolts fall, then he shall recite one Rik-verse (in case he studies the RV.), or one Yajus (in case he studies Yajur-Veda), or one Saman (in case he studies the Sama-Veda) or (without having regard to his particular Veda, the following Yajus), "Bhuh, Bhuvah, Svah, in faith I offer true devotion". Then, forsooth, his daily recitation is accomplished thereby for that day[1] (2/I/:46).

If that is done (if the passage of VB. is combined with that quoted in the Sutra 5) the former stands not in contradiction with the decision of the Aryas. For they (who know the law) teach both the continuance and the interruption (of the daily recitation of the Veda). The precepts are founded on a passage of the Veda and have only a religious motive -- and there is no worldly motive perceptible in their (Aryas) motives. So it refers only to the repetition of the sacred texts in order to learn them not to their application at sacrifices. (Why the decision of the Aryas presupposes the existence of a Vedic passage -- the answer is) : All precepts were (originally) taught in the Brahmanas (but these texts havc been lost). Their existence is inferred from their usage (2/I/:45-47). By way of laudation they (five yajnas) are called 'great sacrifices' or 'great sacrificial sessions' (2/I/:48).

In (II-9, 21) the APDS. states that the duty to live in the teacher's house after initiation is common to all four orders, i.e. the householdership, the studentship, the order of ascetics and the order of hermits in the woods. *Not to abandon sacred learning is a duty common to all of them*[2]
(2/I/:151).

---

1. सर्वेषामुपनयनप्रभृति समान आचार्यकुले वासः ।।३।। सर्वेषामनुत्सर्गो विद्यायाः ।।४।।

While stating rules for the ascetic (Sannyasin) who accepts the order after having fulfilled the duties of the student order the APDS. enjoins that he shall live without a fire, without a house, without pleasures, without protection. He must remain silent but *utter speech only on the occasion of the daily recitation of the Veda*[1] (2/I/:152).

Enjoining the rules for the hermit living in the woods it declares that only after completing the studentship that he shall go forth, remaining chaste. He shall keep one fire only, have no house, enjoy no pleasures, have no protection, observe silence, *uttering on the occasion of the daily recitation of the Veda only*[2].

The APDS. following the line of the ShB. and TA. declares the solemn importance of Svadhyaya making it obligatory to all orders. It specifically states that an ascetic (Sannyasin) and a hermit (Vanaprastha) should not abandon Svadhyaya. It accepts Svadhyaya as tapas and 'great sacrifice' or 'great sacrificial session'. Not only that the APDS. applies the term tapas for the code that is prescribed for the studentship, the transgression of which deprives the student of his ability for learning but the student who is upright and forgiving; who is devoted to law (Dharma) and who is dedicated to the rules of studentship attains the perfection.

The GDS. in its Sutra (2/I/:5, 4) enjoins the perpetual performance of Svadhyaya. Haradatta the commentator states that the term नित्य in the Sutra नित्य स्वाध्यायः specifically suggests that Svadhyaya should be performed whenever one finds time and even in the period which is not prescribed for the Brahmayajna (16:47). The GDS. categorically says that while deciding the hierarchy of the persons fit to be honoured, learning should receive the highest importance (2:1/:6, 19). The Sutra also enjoins on the Snataka that he should always occupy himself in the study of the Veda (2/I/:9, 72).

---

1. अथ परिव्राजः ।।७।। अत एव ब्रह्मचर्यवान् प्रव्रजति ।।८।। तस्योपदिशन्ति ।।९।। स्वाध्याय एवोत्सृजमानो वाचं ग्रामे प्राणवृत्तिं प्रतिलभ्यानि होममुत्रश्चरेत् ।।१०।।

2. अथ वानप्रस्थः ।।१८।। अत एव ब्रह्मचर्यवान् प्रव्रजति ।।।१९।। तस्योपदिशन्ति ।।२०।। एकाग्निरनिकेतः स्यादशर्माशरणो मुनिः । स्वाध्याय एवोत्सृजमानो वाचम् ।।२१।।

In the essential qualities of a very learned (well-informed -- बहुश्रुत) person the GDS. enumerates knowledge of the Vedas along with the Vedangas as well as that of the ways of the world and expertise in the special theological discourse, traditional legends and cosmological myths; total engrossment in the acts of study, giving charity and in the act of sacrificing and that of conducting it (2/I/:8, 5, 6, 9, 10).

SVADHYAYA IN THE GRIHYA SUTRAS

The AGS. has a lengthy passage on Svadhyaya or Brahmayajna. The AGS. (II-3, 2-3) is almost the same as the ShB. (XI-5, 6, 4-8) and TA. (II-10-1) except in three respects, viz. in the AGS. the Samans are said to be honey-offerings (ShB. and TA. Soma-offerings); the Atharvanangiras are said to be Soma-offerings (ShB. fat-offerings, TA. honey-offerings) and the Brahmanas, Kalpas, Gathas, Narasamsis, Itihasa and Puranas are said to be oblations of ambrosia (ShB. honey- offerings; TA. fat-offerings).

The passages (III-4, 6-7) of the Sutra have the same connotation as the TA. (II-12 and 15). They run as:

> And it is also understood (in the Shruti),
> 'May he be standing, walking, sitting, or lying (the text belonging to) whatsoever sacrifice he repeats, that sacrifice indeed he has offered'.
> 'Regarding this (Svadhyaya) there are two cases in which the study (of the sacred texts) is forbidden: when he is impure himself, and when the place is' (16/I/:220).

The ShGS. while describing the qualities of a Brahmana who is to be invited for giving food at the end of the sacrificial acts states[1] that voice, form, age, learning, moral character and

---

1. वाग्रूपवयः श्रुतशीलवृत्तानि गुणाः ।।२।। श्रुतं तु सर्वानत्येति ।।३।।न श्रुत मतीयात् ।।४।।

अधिदैवमथाध्यात्ममधियज्ञमिति त्रयम् । मन्त्रेषु ब्राह्मणे चैव श्रुतमित्यमिधीयते ।।५।।

क्रियावन्तमधीयानं श्रुतवृद्धं तपस्विनम् । भोजयेत् तं सकृद्यस्तु न तं भूयः क्षुदश्नुते ।।६।।

यां तितर्पयिषेत् काञ्चिद्देवतां सर्वकर्मसु । तस्या उद्दिश्य मनसा दद्यादेवं विधाय वै ।।७।।

नैवं विधे हविर्न्यस्तं न गच्छेद्देवतां क्वचित् । निधिरेष मनुष्याणां देवानां पात्रमुच्यते ।।८।।

(right) conduct are the qualities required but learning,. however, outweighs every other qualification, and so the Sutra enjoins that a learned one should not be passed over (16/I/:15-16).

The threefold knowledge refers to the knowledge of deities; of the Atman and that of the sacrifice which have been handed down in the Mantras and in the Brahmanas. This is called learning. The person who is a performer of sacred rites who has studied the Veda, who is old in learning and devoted to austerities is called -- treasure of men, vessel of gods. So food given to such a person will never miss its way to the diety which the sacrificer wants to satiate. Not only that, 'He who gives food even once to such (a learned one), hunger will not befall that man any more (16/I/:16).

In (I-4, 1-2) the ShGS. states that 'when he has risen in the morning and has sipped water, let him perform his Svadhyaya daily'. It also gives list of hymns and verses of the Veda that are to be recited in the Svadhyaya.

The BOGS. in (II-9, 4-6) enjoins to repeat the Gayatri Mantra and to study the Veda, etc. and also the verses (VS.XX, 14-16). It also states that what a person studies is his Brahmayajna.

In order to emphasize as to why a Brahmana should continue his study day by day without interruption, the KauGS. gives twenty-six reasons[1] (III-12, 1-33):

---

1. तद्यथा कुले जातः । ।२ । । शक्तिमान् । ।३ । । पूर्वे चाभिरूपा आसन् । ।४ । । साध्वाचरितं चैतत् । ।५ । । ऋणं चैतद् ब्राह्मणस्य । ।६ । । कर्मणामध्ययनं शुभतरम् । ।७ । ।अधीत्य च कार्याकार्ये ज्ञास्यामि । ।८ । । विद्वांसश्च सर्वत्र पूज्यन्ते । ।९ । । शिष्यांश्च शृश्रुषन्ते । ।१० । । महयन्ति च सर्वत्र । ।११ । । सर्वत्र गतिमान् भविष्यामि । ।१२ । । यक्ष्यामि । ।१३ । । याजयिष्यामि । ।१४ । । लक्षणीयो भविष्यामि । ।१५ । । हवींषि च सुसंस्कृतानि भोक्ष्यामि । ।१६ । । मया च स्वाध्यायवता माता पितरौ स्वर्गे लोके सुखमेधिष्येते । ।१७ । । ब्रह्मचर्येण चायुष्मान् वर्चस्वी भविष्यामि । ।१८ । । स्वाध्यायेन क्षिप्रंपाप्मानमपहन्यामिति च । ।१९ । । स्वाध्यायवतः सर्वे लोकाः । ।२० । । नाप्राप्यं तस्य किञ्चित् । ।२१ । । न तस्य पुनरावृत्तिः । ।२२ । । मन्त्रब्राह्मणयोः वेदशब्दः । ।२३ । । वेदो हि धर्ममूलम् । ।२४ । । अचोरहरणीयं च ब्रह्म । ।२५ । । एकैकाचर्क् सम्यगधीता कामधुग्भवति । ।२६ । । यं यं क्रतुमधीते तेन तेन चेष्टं भविष्यति । ।२७ । । तदपिश्लोकाः । ।२८ । ।
केतुमान् ऴधिमान् दक्षो मित्रवान् धृतिमान् शुचिः । शीलवान् श्रुतवान् दान्तो भवेद्वै पङ्क्ति-पावनः' । ।२९ । ।
चोरराजन्युदकेभ्यः सदा सञ्चयिनां भयम् । निर्भयास्तु सुखं वैद्याश्चान्त्यक्षय्य वृत्तायः । ।३० । ।

1. As he is born in the family (of the learned) (so it becomes obligatory for him).
2. As he possesses the competence (to study) (and that competence should not remain useless).
3. As it is corresponding with the tradition of his family (where Svadhyaya continued uninterrupted).
4. As it is an upright conduct.
5. This being the debt of the Brahmana.
6. Among all the acts study is more auspicious.
7. Only by studying that I will know what is doable and what is not.
8. Learned are honoured in all places.
9. Pupils remain attentive (to the teacher).
10. (Because of his learning) one is valued greatly.
11. (Because of my learning) I will have access anywhere.
12. (It is with the knowledge of trayi vidya that) I can conduct the acts of sacrifice.
13. (Also) I can perform the office of the sacrificing priest.
14. (It is on account of my learning that) I will be a distinguished (person).
15. I will eat refined oblations.
16. I being devoted to self-learning, my parents will rejoice in heaven.
17. Because of celibacy I will have vigour and will have long-life.
18. By (my) Svadhyaya I will expiate sin immediately.
19. All worlds are (easily) accessible to the person who performs Svadhyaya (regularly).
20. Nothinig is impossible for him.
21. To him there is no return to worldly existence.
22. The term Veda is applied to the Mantra and Brahmana (portions).
23. The Veda is the source of Dharma.
24. This Brahman or knowledge could not be robbed off by a thief.

25. The study of a single hymn (of the Veda, here RV.) becomes a fabulous cow yielding all desires.
26. Whatever noble thoughts I learn, they in turn will grant me wishes.

The KauGS. further states that -- in this connection there are (the following) verses: (28).

> (The स्वाध्यायिन्) who is renowned and who is possessed of food, friends and courage; who is pious, noble, prompt and proficient in the sacred knowledge, would become sanctifier of the company (29). Only the hoarders have always fear from the king, thief, water and fire but the learned (persons) are fearless as they have inexhaustible means of subsistence, they live comfortably (30).
>
> Therefore, in this way, much has been said about the purpose of the knowledge of the Veda. So the truthful and self- possessed should try to engage himself in study (31).
>
> At the end of the section a RV. hymn[1] is quoted: Him who is ever vigilant, holy verses desire: to him who is ever vigilant sacred songs proceed : him who is ever vigilant the Soma thus addresses : I am ever abiding in thy fellowship
> (RV. V 44, 14; 19/III/231).

Svadhyaya in Vaikhanasasmartasutra

In (VI-17) the VSS. states that the obligatory sacrifice to Brahman consists in muttering to oneself either the first three chapters of the Samhita or the opening chapters of the four Vedas : In (IX-13) the Sutra says that when the person is going to perform the Brahmayajna or Svadhyaya he should recite as his obligatory pensum of recitation, the Yajussamhita, as far as he likes, beginning: "For force thee, for strength thee (or only) the first three chapters. As occasional recitation he should recite

1. तदेतत्पुष्कलं वाक्यं वेदज्ञानप्रयोजनम्। कुर्यादध्ययने यत्नं सत्यवादी जितेन्द्रियः ।।३१।।
यो जागार तमृचः कामयन्ते यो जागार त मु सामानियान्ति। योजागार तमयं सोम आह तवाहमस्मि सख्ये न्योकाः इति।।३३।।

the (twelve) hymns beginning "Right and truth. Or he may recite (instead of Yajussamhita) the opening parts of each of the Vedas. It further states that the 'sacrifice to Brahman' is the beginning of all sacrifice. Therefore, it should be performed by the twice-born from their initiation (4:211).

SVADHYAYA IN THE SMRITIS

The Manu Smriti in (II:104-107) enjoins that he who desires to perform Svadhyaya, may even recite the Savitri near water,. retiring into the forest, controlling his organs and concentrating his mind. Both when one studies the supplementary treatises of the Veda, and when one recites the daily portion of the Veda, no regard need be paid to forbidden days. Likewise when (one repeats) the sacred texts required for a burnt oblation. There are no forbidden days for the daily recitation, since that is declared to be a Brahmasattra (a perpetual sacrifice offered to Brahman), at that the Veda takes the place of the burnt oblations, and it is meritorious (even), when (natural phenomena, requiring) a cessation of the Veda-study, take the place of the exclamation Vashat. For him who, being pure and controlling his organs, during a year daily recites the Veda according to the rule, that (daily recitation) will even cause sweet and sour milk, clarified butter and honey to flow (3:49).

> In (II:166-167) Manu states that:
>
> "Let a Brahmana who desires to perform austerities,. constantly repeat the Veda; for the study of the Veda is declared (to be) in this world the highest austerity for a Brahmana[1] (3:60-61).

Manu further says that the twice-born man performs the highest austerity upto the extremities of his nails, who, though wearing a garland, daily recites the Veda in private to the utmost of his ability.

While stating the rules for the Snataka Manu enjoins that the Snataka should avoid all means of acquiring wealth which

1. वेदमेव सदाभ्यस्येत्तपस्तपस्यन्द्विजोत्तमः । वेदाभ्यासो हि विप्रस्य तपः परमिहोच्यते । ।१६६ । ।
आ हैव सनखाग्रेभ्यः परमं तप्यते तपः । यः स्त्रग्व्यपि द्विजोऽधीते स्वाध्यायं शक्तितोऽन्वहम् । ।१६७ । ।

would impede the study of the Veda. Let him maintain himself anyhow but study as his dedication to the study of the Veda secures the realization of his aims (II-17). He enjoins on the hermit in the forest that he should always be industrious in his Svadhyaya (VI:8). Even to the ascetic he emphasizes the study of the Vedas constantly as that is the refuge of the ignorant, and even that of those who know the meaning of the Veda. Manu also maintains that the study of the Vedas is the protection of those who seek endless beautitude (VI:83-84). The Vishnu Smriti (XXX:34-38)[1] states that a person who studies the hymns of the RV.(regularly) feeds the manes with clarified butter; he who studies the Yajus texts feeds them with honey; he who studies the Saman melodies feeds them with milk; he who studies the Atharva- Veda feeds them with meat and he who studies the Puranas, Itihasas, Vedangas and the Institutes of the Sacred Law, feeds them with rice (8:126).

Like Manu the Smriti enjoins that the Snataka should not get engaged in any work that would impede the study and teaching of the Veda (LXXI:4)[2]. The Smriti also says that a hermit must not relinquish Svadhyaya (XLIV-6)[3].

The Yajnavalkya Smriti declares that "for the twice-born, of all the auspicious acts, it is the study of the Veda that is considered to be the best bestower of the highest bliss (I-2, 40). The Smriti further states that the person who studies the hymns of RV. daily, satisfies the gods with honey and milk and feeds the manes with honey and clarified butter. He who studies the Yajus-texts daily, satisfies the gods with clarified butter and amrosia and feeds the manes with honey and clarified butter. He who studies the Saman melodies daily, satisfies the gods with Soma and clarified butter and feeds the manes with honey and clarified butter.

---

1. तत्र च यद् ऋचो ऽधीते तेनास्याजेन पितृणां तृप्तिर्भवति ।।३४।। यद् यजूंषि तेन मधुना ।।३५।। यत् सामानि तेन पयसा ।।३६।। यद् आथर्वणं तेन मांसेन ।।३७।। यत् पुराणेतिहासवेदाङ्गधर्मशास्त्राण्यधीते तेनास्यान्नेन ।।३८।।

2. स्वाध्यायविरोधि कर्म नाचरेत् ।।४।।

3. स्वाध्यायं च न जहयात् ।।६।।

He who studies the Atharvangiras daily, according to his ability, satisfies the gods with fat and the manes with honey and clarified butter. And he who studies daily the (special) theological discourses, the traditional myths, the Narasamsi Gathas, the histories and the sciences to the best of his ability, satisfies the gods with meat, milk and rice and feeds the manes with honey and clarified butter. The twice-born who performs Svadhyaya day by day without interruption gains the merit of giving earth thrice in charity replete with wealth (I-2, 41-48). The Smriti advises the Snataka not to desire anything that would stand as an impediment to Svadhyaya (I-6, 129). The Smriti enjoins on the hermit to be engrossed in Svadhyaya day by day (III-3, 48).

THE METHOD OF SVADHYAYA

TA. II-11 specifically describes how and where Brahmayajna or Svadhyaya is to be performed. A person who wants to perform Brahmayajna should repair to a place so far away to the east, north or north-east of his village that the thatch covering houses is not visible and when the sun rises he should wear his sacred thread (in the Upavita form) under his right arm, should sit down on a pure spot, should wash both his hands with water, should sip water thrice, should wipe his hand twice with water, should once sprinkle his lips with water, and touch his head, eyes,. nostrils, ears and heart; he should spread out a large seat of darbhas, should be seated facing the east with his legs crossed over each other (the left foot being underneath and the right foot on the left thigh) and then should repeat his Veda; (it is said that) the darbhas are indeed the flavour (or sweetness) of waters and herbs; he (by sitting on darbhas) makes his Veda full of sweetness. Placing his left hand on the right knee with the palm turned up and covering it with the right hand the palm of which is turned down and placing blades of darbha between both hands, he should begin with the syllable 'Om' which is a Yajus, whch is representative of the three Vedas, which is all speech, and is the highest syllable; this has been declared by a hymn of RV.[1] (I-164, 39) :

ऋचो अक्षरे परमे व्योमन्यस्मिन्देवा अधिविश्वे निषेदुः ।
यस्तन्नवेद किमृचा करिष्यति य इत्त द्विदुस्त इमे समासते ।।

He recites the syllables ॐ भूः भूवः स्वः ; he thereby has employed the truth of speech. Then he recites thrice the Gayatri verse,

1. All the gods have taken their seats upon this supreme heaven, the imperishable (text) of the Veda: What will he, who knows not this, do with the Veda? but they who do know it, are perfect

which is addressed to Savitru, by its feet separately, then by half of it, then the whole verse without stopping. The sun is the creator of glory, he secures glory itself; then he begins (the next day) the repetition of the Vedic texts from that point which he had noted (the previous day)[1]. The TA. explicitly declares that a person should necessarily perform Svadhyaya daily without fail, the posture, time and place are quite subordinate.

The TA. further states that he should conclude the Brahmayajna by repeating thrice the verse :[2]

नमो ब्रह्मणे नमो अस्त्वग्नये नमः पृथिव्यै नमः ओषधीभ्यः ।
नमो वाचे नमो वाचस्पतये नमो विष्णवे बृहते करोमि ।।

Then he shoud sip water and return home, thereafter whatever he gives becomes the fees of the sacrifice (9/II/I; 702-03).

The AGS. (III:2-2 - III:3-4) gives almost the same procedure of Svadhyaya with a little difference in one or two points. The AGS. enjoins that one should recite gazing at the horizon or one may close one's eyes or one may look in such a way that one feels that one can concentrate one's mind. According to the AGS. the shortest Svadhyaya would be ॐ भू: भूव: स्व: ; the Gayatri verse repeated thrice; then at least one hymn of the RV. and then the verse 'नमो ब्रह्मणे' (quoted above) repeated thrice. The AGS. mentions -- four Vedas, Brahmanas, Kalpas, Gathas, Narasamsis, Itihasa and Purana for study but also says that one may recite only as much as one feels that one can afford to do with a concentrated mind.

According to ShGS, the Svadhyaya is accompanied by the following text:

> To-day, god Savitar (RV. V:82, 4-5); the hymn, 'Go away, Manaspati' (X-164); the hymn, 'Right and truth' (X-

---

1. The idea is that one is not to begin to recite the Vedic texts at random. When a man has recited a portion of any Veda one-day, he should note where he stopped and continue his recitation next day from that point (9:702).

2. Adoration to Brahma, to Agni, to the earth, to herbs to speech, to the Lord of Speech, I offer adoration to the great Vishnu.

> 190); the verses: 'Look down, ye Adityas' to end of the hymn (VIII: 47, 11-18); the verse 'O Indra, the best treasures' (II-21, 6); the verse, 'Adoration to the great ones' (I-27, 13); the verse, 'Where we fear, Indra' (VIII-50, 13); the verse, 'And of the sleep' (I-120, 12); the verse, 'He who says to me, O King' (II-28, 10); the hymn, 'Let glory be mine, Agni' (M- 128); and the five verses, 'Bliss may create for us' (V-51, 11 seq.) (I-4).

The Vaikhanasasmartasutra states that:

> Having strewn grass on a clean spot and having assumed the sitting posture sacred to Brahman, holding a strainer in his (right) hand, and making the anjali sacred to Brahman, he should recite, with his face directed to the east, first the Savitru verse, and, then, as obligatory recitation, the chapters beginning: "For food thee, for strength thee", as far as he likes. As occasional recitation, he should recite the chapters beginning" "Right and truth"; "From the evil done to the Gods"; "What of me in the womb"; "The gladdening one has moved forward"; "The strainer of the good one"; "To Jata Vedas"; "Of Vishnu now"; "He with the thousand heads"; "One-syllabled"; "I have brougth thee higher"; "Thou, O Agni"; "Be purified". Finally he should address to the sun as many verses as he likes (4:12).

In (II-10) the Sutra refers to the स्वाध्यायसूक्त which contains some of the parts of Samhita which are referred to in (1-4). Caland quotes the Darpana, accordingly these hymns are intended for the Brahmayajna (4:54).

THE FOUR VEDA - VRATAS

Gautama enumerates four Veda-Vratas among the Sanskaras (VIII-15) but according to Kane (9/I/:370) their names and procedures differ considerably in the several Grihya sutras. These special Vratas, the Vedic student has to undergo or rather which he may undergo in the time of studentship. Some Grihya sutras like PGS. state nothing about them. The AGS. states an omnibus rule that in these Vratas all the ceremonies starting from shaving the head upto Paridana[1] that are performed at the Upanayana are repeated each time with each Vrata (I-22-20). These Vratas accordingly are Mahanamni, Mahavrata (AA, I and V), Upanishad and Godana.

Each Vrata is to be performed for a year.

The ShGS. mentions four Vratas as Shukriya, Shakvara, Vratika and Aupanishada. First comes the Savitri verse for which the student prepares himself by observing Savitra- Vrata; this lasts either one year, or three days, or the Savitri can be taught him immediately (V:1-3). Then follows the Shukriya - Vrata[2] of three days, or twelve days, or one year, or any other period of time according to the teacher's pleasure (II-10). By this Vrata the student is enabled to study the main portion of the Veda. Finally come the Shakvara, Vratika, Aupanishada observances, each of which refer to the different parts of the Aranyaka (16/I/:8). The ShGS, also states that the Shakvara (observance), is to be kept one year so also the Vratika and Aupanishada observances (II:11-12). At the beginning of each of these Vratas there is a separate Upanayana, followed by a ceremony called Uddikshanika (giving up the preparatory observances) and then the Vrata is to be performed for one year.

---

1. AGS. I: 19,8 tO I:20-7.

2. शुक्रिय शब्दो वेदवाची तत्सम्बधाद् व्रतमपि शुक्रियम्। ।रामचंद्र । ।

(/I/76)

The GGS. (of Samaveda) mentions five Vratas, viz. Godanika, Vratika, Aditya, Aupanishada and Jyeshthasamika-Vrata each of which has to last one year (III/I/28). By the followers of the Samaveda the ceremony of the Godana, or cutting of the beard was put into connection with their system of Vratas : the undergoing of the Godana Vrata enabled the student to study the Purvarchika of the Samaveda. The Vratika-Vrata was introductory to the study of the Aranyaka, with the exclusion of the Shukriya sections; the Aditya-Vrata to the Shukriya sections, the Upanishada-Vrata, to the study of the Upanishad-Brahmana; Jyeshthasamika-Vrata to the study of the Agyadohas. The Sutra prescribes certain observances for the Godana-Vrata such as avoiding falsehood, anger, sexual intercourse, perfumes, dancing and singing, collyrium, honey and meat; not wearing shoes in the village (II/I/15-25). It also says that wearing the girdle, going the rounds for alms, carrying a staff, daily bath, putting a fuel (on the fire), and reverentially saluting (the teacher) in the morning are common to all Vratas (III/I/:27). The KauGS. speaks of the same Vratas as Gobhila (II/5/17). It also states that the Shakvara-Vrata was kept for one year, or for three, or six or nine. The person who keeps the Vrata wears dark clothes, eats dark food, is entirely addicted to his teacher. He should stand in day-time and sit at night (II/5/23-27).

The BOGS. states that there are Vratas of one year each which precede the study of certain Brahmana texts (of the Black Yajus) they are[1] Hotarah, Shukriyas, Upanishadah, Godana and Sammitam (III/II/:4). The Sutra describes them in detail. If the student failed in observing the specific Vratas he had to perform Prayaschitta by undergoing the Prajapatya penance thrice, or six times or twelve times. If he is guilty of failing in his daily duties as a Brahmacharin he had to undergo the penance of three Krucchras and to perform a homa with the Vyahritis separately and together. If he was guilty of other more serious lapses (sexual intercourse with a woman, etc.) he had to undergo heavier penance (9/II/I:373-74).

---

1. अथेमानि ब्राह्मणानि सांवत्सरिकैर्व्रतैरध्येयानि भवन्ति होतारश्शुक्रियाष्युपनिषदो गोदानं सम्मितं इति ।।४।।

THE METHOD OF TEACHING THE VEDA

The ShGS. describes the method as follows[1]: To students who have been duly initiated he shall set forth the Veda. The teacher sits facing the east or north, while the student sits to his right facing the north or two students may sit in that way; but if there are more than two they should sit as there is room for them. The student should not sit on a high seat in presence of a Guru nor on the same seat with him, he should not sit with outstretched feet, nor stretchng his arms under his knees, nor should lean his body against a support, nor should he place his feet like an axe.

After the student has said, 'Recite, Sir'! the teacher shall cause him to pronounce the syllable, 'Om'. 'Om', replies the student. Thereafter the student recites uninterruptedly, when he has recited he embraces his teacher's feet and says, "We have finished, Sir!" and (goes away) according to his business. Some teachers say that the teacher should say, "Leave, let us stop".

In the RV. Pratishakhya (15) there is also a description of the method of teaching the Veda, which closely agrees with the passages of the ShGS as quoted above. It adds that the teacher may also sit facing the north-east. When the teacher recites two

---

1. न्यायोपेतेभ्यश्च वर्तयेत् । ।१ । । प्राङ्वोदङ् वासी न आचार्यो दक्षिणत उदङ्मुख इतरः । ।२ । । द्वौ वा । ।३ । । भूयांसस्तु यथावकाशम् । ।४ । । नोऽच्छ्रितासनोपविष्टो गुरुसमीपे । ।५ । । नैकासनस्थः । ।६ । । न प्रसारित पादः । ।७ । । न बाहुभ्यां जानूप संगृह्य । ।८ । । नोपाश्रित शरीरः । ।९ । । नोपस्थकृत पादः । ।१० । । न पाद कुठारिकां कृत्वा । ।११ । । 'अधीहि भो इति' उक्त्वाऽऽचार्य ॐ ङ्कारं प्रचोदयेत् । ।१२ । । ॐ इतीतरः प्रतिपद्यते । ।१३ । । तत्सन्तत मधीयीत । ।१४ । । आधीत्योपसंगृह्य । ।१५ । । "विरताः स्म भो इति" उक्त्वा यथार्थम् । ।१६ । । विसृष्टं विराम स्तावदिति एके । ।१७ । ।नाधीयता मन्तरा गच्छेत् । ।१८ । । नात्मानं विपरिहरेदधीयान'ः । ।१९ । । यदि चेद्दोषः स्यात्भि गत्रमुपोष्या ऽहो रात्रं वा सावित्रीमभ्यावर्तयेद्या वच्छकनुयाद् ब्राह्मणेभ्यः किञ्चिद् दद्यादहोरात्रमुरम्य प्राध्यायनम् । ।२० । ।

words or more, the first pupil (to the right of the teacher) repeats the first of the two or more words and the other pupils repeat the rest afterwards. The teacher recites one word if it is a compound, two words if they are uncompounded; the teacher also clearly explains how to recite the words if there is any difficulty; in this way the whole Prashna is finished and all the pupils repeat again the whole of it. A Prashna generally has three mantras and each adhyaya has about sixty Prashnas.

Manu states that (II:70-74; 2:43) a student who is to begin the study of the Veda, shall receive instruction, after he has sipped water in accordance with the Institutes, has made the Brahmanjali (joining the palms for the sake of Veda), has put on a clean dress, and has brought his organs under due control. At the beginning and at the end of a lesson he must always clasp both the feet of his teacher, and he must study, joining his hands; that is called the Brahmanjali. With crossed hands he must clasp the feet of the teacher, and touch the left (foot) with his left hand, the right foot with his right hand. To him who is about to begin studying, the teacher, always unwearied, must say: Ho, recite! He shall leave off when the teacher says: Let a stoppage take place. He should repeat the syllable Om at the beginning and at the end of a lesson in the Veda. GGS. (I:49-58) also gives similar rules.

The study of the Veda did not merely consist in learning the mantra by heart but one had also to understand the meaning. The Nirukta (I-18) states that that person who having studied the Veda, does not know its meaning, is indeed a tree, a mere carrier of a load. The person who knows the meaning secures all happiness; his sins being shaken off by knowledge, he reaches heaven. Kane quotes Daksha as, "the study of Veda involves five things, viz. first committing to memory the Veda, then reflection over its meaning, keeping it fresh by repeating it again and again, japa and imparting it to the pupils" (9/II/I:357). Manu (XII-103) says that those who have committed to memory the Veda are more distinguished than the ignorant, those who possess a knowledge of the Veda are more distinguished than those who only remember the words, men who follow the precepts surpass those who merely know their meaning. The real purpose of the study of the Veda is the knowledge about religious actions that it conveys and not only to commit them to memory (9/II/I:357).

THE UPAKARMA UTSARGA AND ANADHYAYA

Upakarma - The opening of the Vedic term

The Vedic term commenced with the Upakarma ceremony which was to be performed some time during the bright fortnight of the month of Shravana when the herbs appear or under the Hasta Nakshatra or on the full-moonday of Shravana or on the fifth of that month. "The Shravana Nakshatra is evidently considered as particularly fit for this occasion, perhaps because its name is derived from the same root that gives us 'Shruti'. The Hasta Nakshatra is also selected perhaps because Savitri is the presiding deity over Hasta" (1:185).

The procedure of the ceremony of Upakarma is slightly different in the different Grihya Sutras but the main elements appear to be: (1) a sacrifice and a reciting of the Savitri as at the Upanayana, (2) offering of oblations of fried barley and grains with curds and partaking of them, (3) and a recitation of the Veda with the pupils, either in entirety or the first verses only (1:186).

Utsarga Ceremony

After the Upakarma ceremony, the Vedic study goes on for four months and a half or five months and a half or six months and then follows the ceremony of Utsarga or the formal closing of the first Vedic term which is performed according to ShGS. on the first day of the bright fortnight of Magha or on the eighth day of the dark fortnight of Magha or in the month of Pausha under the Nakshatra Rohini (according to Paraskara Grihya Sutra) or in the full-moon of Pausha which is considered as coinciding approximately, with the beginning of the Uttarayana. The teacher and the pupil go to the north-east or in an easterly or northerly direction and there, in a place covered with herbs, they murmur the hymns sacred to the sun and throw clod of earth on the ground to the different quarters of the horizon from the left to the right. Then they go to the brink of a stream, the level of water in which is higher than their secret parts, which is pleasant and has a pleasant bathing-place; and diving into it, perform three suppressions of breath with the Agha-marshana hymns. Holding Darbha-blades in their hands they bathe, reciting three prescribed verses, giving the Darbha blades to each other and pretending to try to take them from each other. They should next satiate by pouring out water the metres, the Rishis, the teachers ancient and modern, the Gandharvas and the fathers. Then they arrange on a pure spot that is inclined towards the east, seats of eastward-pointed Darbha grass, so that they end in the north for the divine beings beginning with Brahman and ending with the Angirasas. They also prepare seats each for his own parental and maternal ancestors and offer water, perfumes, flowers, etc. to them. Having worshipped them next, having put wood on the fire, to the west of the spot in which he has performed the Tarpana and having performed the rites down to the Vyahriti oblations they plant Durva grass on the banks of the stream. They then stir up waves in the water and run a race in an easternly and northernly direction until they lose their breath and when they have returned from the whole ceremony to the village, they offer cakes, coarsely ground grains, and boiled rice to the Brahmanas. The same rites are repeated when they have finished the study of the whole Veda with the exception of the planting of Durva grass, the stirring up of the water and the race (1:187-89).

Interruption of Study - Anadhyaya

This almost year-long recitation of the Vedas was subject to numerous breaks. These breaks took place at the time of the Upakarma and Utsarga for three days. Breaks were due to deaths and births in relations and on the death of the Guru; also on the death of the ruler of the country or on the death of a reverential person. The breaks were caused due to natural phenomena, viz. lighting, thunder or heavy rain, earthquakes, sun or moon eclipse, etc. The regular breaks were -- on the fourteenth days (of the bright and dark fortnight); on new- and full-moon days on the last nights and days of each season, on the days of the ancient Vedic Chaturmasya sacrifices in Kartika, Phalguna and Ashadha (three days), on the Uttarayana and when a new season begins (1:190-92).

The multiplicity of such interruptions need not cause any surprise as the educators of the time had to err on the safe side in guarding the correct and scientific method of recitation of the Vedas down to the minutest part of it because the Vedic texts were not available in written form (1:189).

It was expected that a person who performs Svadhyaya must be heatlhy (not suffering any physical pain) and free from impurity. It was also enjoined that if any of these interruptions stand against the will of the student, let him resume his study after having held his breath and looked at the sun (1:192).

FINDINGS

(1) Spiritual pre-eminence resulting from sacred knowledge was the prime ideal of Brahmanas.

(2) The solemn ritual that would lead to this ideal was Svadhyaya.

(3) Svadhyaya was considered as sacrifice to the Brahman.

(4) The earliest mention of Svadhyaya is found in the ShB.

(5) Svadhyaya was obligatory on the twice-born as he is born as (owing) a debt to the Rishis.

(6) The ShB. gives a comprehensive list of subjects that are to be studied in the Svadhyaya.

(7) Svadhyaya was considered to be the highest sacrifice and penance, the bestower of the highest bliss.

(8) The TA. has identical passages to the ShB. passages in the eulogy to Svadhyaya.

(9) Svadhyaya was considered to be obligatory on all the Ashramas (all orders - including Sannyasa).

(10) It was expected that one should study his lesson dayby day without any interruption - time, place and posture being quite subordinate.

(11) Svadhyaya should be practised even on those days on which the first learners should not study the Veda.

(12) It was asserted that 'the joy of the Shrotriya -- an accomplished student of the Veda is equal to the highest joy possible.

(13) The student of all three Vedas being called tri- Shukriya or tri-Shukra.

(14) The reward of learning was gaining of the title of Kavi, Vipra or sage.

(15) The Dharmashastras too corroborate the same view regarding the Svadhyaya as described in the ShB. and the TA. The ADS. extensively dealt with this subject.

It specifically states that 'not to abandon sacred learning is a duty common to all four orders'.

(16) According to ADS. the term tapas was applied to the observances of the rules of studentship.

(17) The GDS. categorically states that in the hierarchy of the persons fit to be honoured, learning should receive the highest importance.

(18) The Grihya Sutras also sustain the same view regarding Svadhyaya as described in the ShB. and TA. The ASG. has identical passages to the ShB. and the TA.

(19) The ShGS. gives prime importance to learning while describing the qualities of a Brahmana. The Sutra describes the person who is old in the learning and devoted to austerities as treasure of men and vessel of gods.

(20) Manu and Yajnavalkya confirm Svadhyaya as an everlasting sacrifice offered to the Brahman and repeat the same eulogy to Svadhyaya as described in the ShB. and the TA.

(21) The Manu, the Yajnavalkya and the Vishnu Smriti specifically state that a Snataka should avoid all means of acquiring wealth which impede the study of the Veda.

(22) The TA., the AGS. and the ShGS, give specific instructions regarding the method of Svadhyaya.

(23) There are four Veda-Vratas which the Vedic student may undergo in the time of studentship.

(24) The ShGS., RV. Pratishakhya and Manu give specific instructions regarding the method of teaching the Veda.

(25) The opening of the annual course of study is referred to as Upakarma while the end of term as Utsarga. Interruptions of study are called Anadhyayas.

CONCLUSION

The two verses of the RV. referred to in the Brihaddevata (IX:67, 31-32) where it is mentioned that a person who reads the essence stored by Rishis, the Pavamani hymns tastes purified food made sweet by Matarishvan's touch and Sarasvati draws forth for him water, milk and meat. If these verses of the RV. refer to the student of recitation, Svadhyaya has a very deep root in our ancient culture going back to RV. The TS. considers studentship as debt to Rishis or to culture and so the person who perpetually continues his Svadhyaya was designated as "Rishis' treasure warden".

To preserve the institution of Yajna and the vast bulk of the Vedic literature, literary education was transmitted by word of mouth from teacher to pupil -- that is to say the process of imparting knowledge of the sacred hymnology and sacrificial ritual was systematized gradually. To perpetuate this fund of knowledge, self-study or Svadhyaya was made obligatory to all orders of the society giving it the status of Brahmayajna which was to be carried on without any interruption with the exception when the performer is impure himself, and when the place is impure.

The prime ideal of the Brahmanas was to obtain preeminence in Brahmavarchasam -- spiritual pre-eminence resulting from sacred knowledge and the solemn ritual that would surely lead to this ideal was Svadhyaya continued perpetually. So the merits of Svadhyaya were considered unmatched by any other rites and it was confirmed that "Svadhyaya is the bestower of highest bliss".

ShB. gives comprehensive list of subjects for the perusal in Svadhyaya. So the term Svadhyaya has comprehensive reference. It is a contemplative study carried on day by day, without interruption.

The person who is prompt and proficient in the sacred knowledge becomes sanctifier of the company and has inexhaustible means of subsistence. So it is expected that the truthful and self-possessed should try to engage himself in studies because, 'Him who is ever-vigilant (in his studies), holy verses desire : to him who is ever-vigilant, sacred songs proceed : him who is ever-vigilant the Soma thus addresses -- I rest and have my dwelling in your firendship'.

REFERENCES

1. V.M. Apte, *Social and Religious Life In The Grihya Sutras*. Bombay : Popular, 1954.
2. Geroge Buhler. *Apastambas Aphorisms On the Sacred Law Of The Hindus*. Poona : S.K. Belvalkar, Bhandarkar O.R. Institute, 1932.
3. ——————. *The Sacred Laws Of The Aryas*. Delhi : Motilal Banarasidass (Sacred Books of The East Series, in two parts), 1965.
4. W. Caland (Translator). *Vaikhanasasmartasutra*. Delhi : Ramananda Vidhya Bhavan, 1982.
5. Julius Eggeling (Translator). *The Shatapatha Brahmana*. Motilal Banarasidass (Sacred Books of the East Series, in five parts), 1966.
6. P.K. Gode and C.G. Karve (Editors). *Principal Vaman Shivaram Apte's The Practical Sanskrit-English Dictionary* (in three parts). Poona : Prasad Prakashan; I-1957, II-1958, III-1959.
7. Ralph T.H. Griffith (Translator). *The Hymns Of The Rig-veda*. Delhi : Motilal Banarasidass, 1986.
8. Julius Jolly (Translator). *The Institutes Of Vishnu*. Delhi : Motilal Banarasidass, 1986.
9. P.V. Kane, *History Of Dharmashastras* (Vol. II, Part I; Vol. II, Part II). Poona : Bhandarkar Oriental Research Institute, 1941.
10. A.B. Keith (Translator). *The Veda Of The Black Yajus School entitled Taittiriya Samhita* (in two parts). Delhi : Motilal Banarasidass, 1967.
11. A.A. MacDonell and A.B. Keith. *Vedic Index* (two volumes). Varanasi : Motilal Banarasidass, 1958.
12. A.A. MacDonell. *The Brihaddevata* (in two parts). New York : Harvard University, 1904.

13. R.C. Majumdar and A.D. Puralkar (Editors). *The Vedic Age*. London : Geroge Allen and Unwin Ltd., 1951.

14. Max Muller F. (Translator). *The Upanishads* (in two parts). Delhi : Motilal Banarasidass (Sacred Books Of The East), 1965.

15. Monier-Williams. *A Sanskrit-English Dictionary*. Delhi : Motilal Banarasidass, 1986.

16. Hermann Oldenberg (Translator). *The Grihya Sutras* (in two parts). Delhi : Motilal Banarasidass (The Sacred Books Of The East), 1964.

17. U.C. Pandey (Translator). *Gautama Dharmasutra*. Varanasi : Chaukhamba, 1966.

18. Raja Radhakantdev. *Shabdakalpadruma* (Vol.5). Delhi : Motilal Banarasidass, 1961.

19. H.H. Wilson (Translator). *Rigveda Samhita* (in four volumes). Poona : Ashtekar and Co.; I-1946, II-1925, III- 1926, IV-1927.

BIBLIOGRAPHY

Primary Sources

Vedas

(1) Agashe Kashinath Shastri (Editor). *Yajurveda (Taittiriya Samhita of the Black Yajurveda)*. Poona : H.N. Apte, Anandashram Series, No. 42, in eight volumes (with the commentary of Sayanacharya): Vol. I - 1900, Vol. II - 1901, Vol. III - 1901, Vol. IV - 1901, Vol. V - 1902, Vol. VI - 1903, Vol. VII - 1904, Vol. VIII - 1905.

(2) Bapat D.G. (Editor). *Yajurveda (Vaj. Madhyandina Samhita)* with Marathi Translation, Part I and II. Satara : Raja of the Aundha State, 1941.

(3) Satvalekar S.D. (Editor). *Yajurveda (Kthaka Samhita)*. Aundha : Swadhyaya Mandala, 1943.

(4) ———————. (Editor). *Yajurveda (Maitrayani Samhita)*. Aundha : Swadhyaya Mandala, 1943.

Brahmanas

(5) Bapat D.G. (Editor and Translator). *Aitereya Brahmana*, Part I and II. Satara (Panch-vad) : D.G. Bapat, 1942.

(6) Shastri Chinnaswami and Pattabhirama Shastri (Editors). *Tandyamahabrahmana* (with the commentary of Sayanacharya). Banaras : The Chowkhamba (in two parts); I- 1935, II-1936.

(7) Goyanka I.M. (Editor). *Shatapatha Brahmana* (Madhyandina Shakha), Part I. Kashi : Gaurishankar Goyanka, 1937.

(8) Chhaya G.V. (Editor). *Shankhyayana Brahmana*. Poona : H.N. Apte, Anandashrama Series, No. 65, 1911.

(9) Godbole Narayanshastri (Editor). *Taittiriya Brahmana* (with commentary of Sayanacharya). Poona : H.N. Apte, Anandashrama Series, No. 37 (in three parts), 1898.

(10) Sharma B.R. (Editor). *Arsheya Brahmana*. Tirupati : Kendriya Sanskrit Vidyapeetha, 1967.

Aranyakas

(11) Phadake Balashastri (Editor). *Aitareya Aranyaka* (with the commentary of Sayanacharya). Poona : H.N. Apte, Anandashrama Series, 1897.

(12) Phadake Balashastri (Editor). *Taittiriya Aranyaka* (with the commentary of Sayanacharya). Poona : H.N. Apte, Anandashrama Series (in two parts); Part-I - 1897, Part-II - 1898.

(13) Shastri A. Mahadeva and K. Rangachari. *Taittiriya Aranyaka* (with the commentary of Bhatta Bhaskara Mishra). Delhi : Motilal Banarasidass, 1985.

(14) Shridhara Shastri and Other Professors of the Deccan College, Poona (Editors). *Shankhyayana Aranyaka*. Poona : V.G. Apte, Anandashrama Series, 1922.

Upanishads

(15) Agashe Kashinathashastri (Editor). *Chhandogyopanishat* (with the commentaries of Anandagiri and Shankara). Poona : H.N. Apte, Anadashrama Series, 1913.

(16) Bhanu C.G. (Editor and Translator). *Chhandogyopanishat* (with the commentary of Shankara, Marathi Translation). Bombay : Damodar Savalaram and Company, 1920.

(17) Pandits at the Anandashrama (Editors). *Thirty-two Upanishads*. Poona : H.N. Apte, Anandashrama Series, 1895.

(18) Shastri A. Mahadeva (Editor and Translator -English). *The Taittiriya Upanishad* (with the commentaries of Shankara, Sureshvara and Vidyaranya). Madras : Samata, 1980.

Dharmasutras

(19) Buhler Geroge (Editor). *Apastamba's Aphorisms On the Sacred Law Of the Hindus*. Poona : S.K. Belvalkar, Bhandarkar O.R. Institute, 1932.

(20) Pandeya Umeshachandra (Editor and Translator - Hindi). *Gautamadharmasutrani* (with the Mitakshara Vritti). *Varanasi : Chowkhamba, 1966.*

Grihyasutras

(21) Chintamani T.R. (Editor). *Kaushitaka* (with the commentary of Bhavatrata). Delhi : Panini, 1982.

(22) Nene Gopalshastri (Editor). *Paraskara* (with the commentaries of Harihar, Gadadhara and Jayarama). Banaras : Chowkhamba, 1925.

(23) Sehgal S.R. (Editor). *Shankhyayana*. Delhi : Munshi Ram Manohar Lal, 1960.

(24) Sharma N.N. (Editor and Translator -English). *Ashvalayana* (with the commentary of Narayana). Delhi : Eastern Book Linkers, 1976.

(25) Shastri R.H. (Editor). *Manava* (with the commentary of Ashtavakra). Delhi : Panini, 1982.

(26) Shastri S.R. (Editor). *Bodhayana*. Delhi : Panini, 1982.

Smritis

(27) Gauda R.S. (Editor and Translator - Hindi). *Yajnavalkya*. Bombay : H.B. Sharma, 1881.

(28) Jolly Julius (Editor). *Vishnu*. Varanasi : Chowkhamba, 1962.

(29) Panshikar V.L. (Editor). *Manu* (with the commentary of Kullukabhatta). Bombay : Pandurang Javaji, 1933.

Other Works

(30) MacDonell A.A. (Editor and Translator - English). *The Brihaddevata* (in two parts). New York - Harvard University, 1904.

(31) Vyasa Yugalkishor (Editor). *Shaunaka's Pratishakhya of the Rigveda*. Benaras : Messers Braj B. Das and Co., 1903.

Dictionaries

(32) Gode P.K. and C.G. Karve (Editors). *Principal Vaman Shivaram Apte's The Practical Sanskrit-English Dictionary* (in three parts). Poona : Prasad Prakashan, Part-I - 1957, Part-II - 1958, Part-III - 1959.

(33) Monier-Williams, *A Sanskrit-English Dictionary*. Delhi : Motilal Banarasidass, 1986.

(34) Raja Radhakantdev. *Shabdakalpadruma*, Vol.5, Delhi : Motilal Banarasidass, 1961.

Translations

(35) Buhler George (Translator - English). *The Sacred Laws Of The Aryas* (in two parts). Delhi : Motilal Banarasidass, 1965.

(36) Buhler Geroge (Translator -English). *The Laws of Manu*. Motilal Banarasidass, 1964.

(37) Caland W. (Translator - English). *Vaikhanasasmartasutra*. Delhi : Ramananda Vidya Bahvan, 1982.

(38) Eggeling Julius (Translator - English). *The Shatapatha Brahmana*. Delhi : Motilal Banarasidass (Sacred Books of the East Series) in five parts, 1966.

(39) Griffith Ralph T.H. (Translator - English). *The Hymns Of The Rigveda*. Delhi : Motilal Banarasidass, 1986.

(40) Jolly Julius (Translator - English). *The Institutes Of Vishnu*. Delhi : Motilal Banarasidass, 1986.

(41) Keith A.B. (Translator). *The Veda Of The Black Yajus School entitled Taittiriya Samhita* (in two parts). Delhi : Motilal Banarasidass, 1967.

(42) Max Muller F. (Translator - English). *The Upanishads* (in two parts). Delhi : Motilal Banarasidass, 1965.

(43) Oldenberg Hermann (Translator - English). *The Grihyasutras* (in two parts). Delhi : Motilal Banarasidass, 1964.

(44) Upadhyaya G.P. (Translator - Hindi). *The Shatapatha Brahmana*. Delhi : The Research Institute of Ancient Scientific Studies; Part-I - 1967, Part-II - 1969.

(45) Wilson H.H. (Translator - English). *The Rigveda Samhita* (in four volumes). Poona : Ashtekar and Co., Part-I - 1946, Part-II - 1925, Part-III - 1926, Part-IV - 1927.

Secondary Sources

(46) Apte V.M. *Social and Religious Life In The Grihya- Sutra*. Bombay : Popular, 1954.

(47) Banerjee S.C. *Dharma Sutras - A Study In Their Origin and Development*. Calcutta : Punthi Pustak, 1962.

(48) Das S.K. *The Educational Sysem Of The Ancient Hindus*. Delhi : Gian Publishing House, 1986.

(49) Kane P.V. *History Of Dharmashastras* (Volume II, Prt I and II). Poona : Bhandarkar O.R. Institute, 1941.

(50) MacDonell A.A. and A.B. Keith, *Vedic Index* (in two volumes). Varanasi : Motilal Banarsidass, 1958.

(51) Majumdar R.C. and A.D. Pusalkar (Editors). *The Vedic Age*. London : George Allen and Unwin Ltd., 1951.

(52) Mookerji R.K. *Hindu Civilization*, Part-I. Bombay : Bhartiya Vidya Bhavan, 1957.

(53) Suryakant. *Vedic Kosha*. Banaras : Banaras Hindu University, 1963.

INDEX